A Review of the Literature on Sexual Assault Perpetrator Characteristics and Behaviors

Sarah Michal Greathouse, Jessica Saunders, Miriam Matthews, Kirsten M. Keller, Laura L. Miller

RAND Project AIR FORCE

RR-1082-AF
October 2015
Prepared for the United States Air Force

Preface

Sexual assault continues to be a pervasive problem, both for society in general and within the military community. To assist the Air Force in its continued efforts to combat sexual assault perpetration within its ranks, we conducted a review of the existing empirical literature on adult perpetrators who commit sexual assault against other adults, with a particular focus on research published in 2000 or later. Our literature search focused on the current state of scientific knowledge and was not limited to studies focusing on military populations. We uncovered a substantial amount of research devoted to understanding sexual assault perpetration, including the common characteristics of perpetrators who commit sexual assault, and behavioral patterns among this group of offenders. This report provides a summary of our findings from the review of this body of literature.

The research reported here was sponsored by the director of Air Force Sexual Assault Prevention and Response (SAPR), the Office of the Vice Chief of Staff (AF/CVS), and the commander of Air Force Recruiting Service (AFRS/CC). It was conducted within the Manpower, Personnel, and Training Program of RAND Project AIR FORCE as part of a fiscal year 2014 study focused on "Enhancing Sexual Assault Prevention and Response Efforts Through a Better Understanding of Perpetrator Behaviors and Risk Factors."

RAND Project AIR FORCE

RAND Project AIR FORCE (PAF), a division of the RAND Corporation, is the U.S. Air Force's federally funded research and development center for studies and analysis. PAF provides the Air Force with independent analyses of policy alternatives affecting the development, employment, combat readiness, and support of current and future aerospace forces. Research is conducted in four programs: Force Modernization and Employment; Manpower, Personnel, and Training; Resource Management; and Strategy and Doctrine. The research reported here was prepared under contract FA7014-06-C-0001.

Additional information about PAF is available on our website: http://www.rand.org/paf.

Contents

Figures and Table

Summary

Sexual assault continues to be a pervasive problem in the United States. One survey estimates that 19 percent of women and 2 percent of men in the United States have been sexually assaulted at some point in their lifetime. Similarly, within the armed forces, 23 percent of women and 4 percent of men service members report having been sexually assaulted during their military service.

To assist the U.S. Air Force in its continued efforts to prevent sexual assault by its service members, we reviewed existing literature on the characteristics and behaviors of adults who commit sexual assault (ranging from coercion to aggression to behaviors meeting the legal definition of rape) against other adults (including that by strangers, acquaintances, and groups of perpetrators).[1] This work has three aims. First, we synthesize what is known about perpetrator risks and behaviors. Second, we highlight important findings within the literature that could guide ongoing and future sexual assault prevention and training efforts within the Air Force. Third, we discuss whether any sexual assault perpetrator screening tools exist that the Air Force could incorporate in recruitment screening of airmen. We found that most research focuses on solitary men who perpetrate assault against women (which we refer to as male-female sexual assault). Nevertheless, we also searched specifically for relevant literature on female sexual assault perpetrators, men who commit sexual assault against other men, and individuals who participate in group sexual assault.

Characteristics of Male Perpetrators Who Sexually Assault Female Victims

The most commonly studied contributors to perpetration of sexual assault can be grouped into those related to experience of child abuse, previous sexual behavior, interpersonal-skill deficits, gender-related attitudes, perceptions of peer behavior, and substance abuse. We discuss each of these below, as well as efforts to assess their effects in confluence.

Child Abuse

Child abuse includes sexual, physical, and emotional abuse, as well as exposure to violence within the home. While some research indicates a relationship between childhood sexual abuse

---

[1] We considered behaviors ranging from sexual coercion (i.e., the use of violence, threats, and/or harassment to obtain sexual gratification) to sexual aggression (the use of violent acts to forcefully obtain sexual gratification), as well as research that focused specifically on behaviors that would meet the legal definition of sexual assault/rape. We also considered the range of possible relationships between perpetrators and victims, including strangers, acquaintances, intimate partners/spouses, and groups of perpetrators who commit sexual assault against strangers or known victims.

and later sexual assault perpetration, overall findings are mixed, and more research is needed to fully explore the mechanisms of this relationship. The link between sexual assault perpetration and childhood physical abuse or exposure to family violence appears to be more established.

Sexual Behavior

Several surveys have found a correlation between self-reported perpetration of sexual violence and number of sexual partners or early initiation of sex. Studies have also identified a significant link between sexual assault perpetration and impersonal attitudes toward sex, defined as practices and beliefs that sex outside a relationship is acceptable. Finally, both cross-sectional surveys and longitudinal surveys following individuals over time have consistently found a history of sexual assault perpetration to be associated with or predictive of additional sexual assault perpetration.

Interpersonal Skills

Several studies have examined whether sexual assault perpetrators display deficits in their interpersonal skills. Some research indicates that sexual assault perpetrators may have insecure attachment styles and lower empathy toward sexual assault victims, as well as misinterpret sexual cues, but overall, research is mixed. Several studies have failed to find an effect of social-skill deficits on adult sexual assault perpetration. More research is needed to clarify the effects of interpersonal-skills deficits and what else may exacerbate difficulties in interpersonal skills.

Gender-Related Attitudes and Cognitions

The role of gender-related attitudes and cognitions has been among the most studied in research on sexual assault perpetration, in part because sexual assault is often conceptualized as an expression of men's anger against women or a method of dominating or controlling women. Several studies have found that men's endorsement of rape myths, hostility toward women, endorsement of traditional gender roles, and hypermasculinity are related to sexual assault perpetration against women.

Perceptions of Peer Attitudes and Behavior

Several studies have found that individuals who perceive their peers as approving of sexual assault are more likely to commit sexual assault. A smaller number of studies have also identified a link between sexual assault perpetration and perceptions of peer pressure to engage in sexual activity.

Substance Use

Previous research estimates that in about half of sexual assaults, the victim, the perpetrator, or both consumed alcohol prior to the assault. Research on the association between alcohol use and sexual assault seems to indicate that alcohol consumption can play a role in sexual assault perpetration. Some studies indicate that alcohol consumption increases misperceptions of female sexual interest.

Research on the association between drug use and sexual assault perpetration is sparse, and more is needed to fully understand the influence of drug use on sexual assault perpetration.

The Confluence Model of Sexual Aggression

Researchers have concluded that sexual assault perpetration is a complex behavior that is likely influenced by a combination of factors, including an individual's developmental and family history, personality, and environmental and societal influences.

The Confluence Model of Sexual Aggression (Malamuth et al., 1991 and 1995), shown in Figure S.1, is one of the most frequently cited and tested theories of adult sexual assault perpetration. It considers developmental, attitudinal, and environmental factors and describes two different pathways to sexual aggression: the hostile-masculinity pathway and the impersonal-sex pathway.

Figure S.1. The Confluence Model of Sexual Aggression

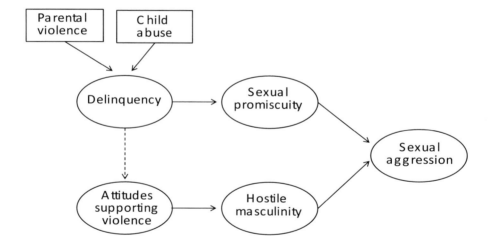

In the hostile-masculinity pathway, the development of negative attitudes and opinions about women leads to sexual aggression. In the sexual-promiscuity pathway, early and increased sexual experiences lead to sexual aggression. While each pathway may independently predict sexual aggression, the Confluence Model also asserts that the pathways can interact to predict sexual aggression. According to the model, individuals who have both high levels of hostile masculinity and high levels of approval for impersonal sex should be most likely to display sexual aggression. The Confluence Model has been tested several times with different populations and has been found to explain about 30 percent of the frequency and severity of sexual aggression

(Hall et al., 2005; Malamuth, 1996; Malamuth et al., 1991 and 1995). Additional research has suggested correlates and precursors to sexual aggression (which includes both legal and illegal behavior), but none is an accurate way to predict who will perpetrate sexual assault at any particular time. Researchers are continuing to work to better explain the etiology of sexual assault perpetration.

Behaviors of Male Perpetrators Who Sexually Assault Female Victims: The Cycle of Sexual Offending

A recent review of the behavior of sexual assault perpetrators contends they engage in a cycle of offending that consists of three stages: (1) planning on a conscious or unconscious level prior to the offense, (2) committing the offense, and (3) forming thoughts after the offense allowing the individual to commit sexual assault again in the future. Although some perpetrators of sexual assault make a series of deliberate decisions about how, when, and where to hunt, target, and subdue a victim, most make a series of seemingly irrelevant decisions that eventually lead to the commission of a sexual assault. For example, a perpetrator may feel lonely or angry and begin drinking to cope with these negative feelings, then go to a bar or club where there are a number of highly intoxicated women, presenting the opportunity to commit sexual assault. Other research has found that perpetrators' behavior during the assault can be very different depending on whether they are strangers or acquaintances of the victim. Following the assault, sexual assault perpetrators commonly display cognitive distortions, or thought processes, that provide justification or excuses for their behavior. These may include blaming the victim or denials that the act was planned.

Female Sexual Assault Perpetrators, Male-on-Male Sexual Assault Perpetrators, and Multiple-Perpetrator Sexual Assault

Research on female sexual assault perpetrators is still emerging, with many fewer studies than on male perpetrators who assault female victims. Most existing research has focused on the characteristics and behaviors of female offenders who commit assaults against children or adolescents. There is little consensus on the characteristics or behaviors of female sexual assault perpetrators.

Similarly, until recently there has been little recognition of sexual assault perpetrated by adult men against other adult men. Relatively few studies have examined the issue, and much of the early research on male-male sexual assault simply described the incidents, rather than comparing perpetrators of such acts with a control group. Studies have generally identified two different types of perpetrators based on their motivations for committing the sexual assault. These are homosexual men who assault other homosexual men primarily for intimacy or sexual gratification, and heterosexual men who assault other men as an expression of social dominance or control. Overall, however, we know very little about the characteristics of these perpetrators, on whom more research is needed.

Finally, multiple-perpetrator sexual assault is that committed by more than one individual. Research on this type of assault is also very limited. Research does indicate that multiple-perpetrator sexual assault offenders tend to be strangers or casual acquaintances of the victim rather than intimate partners. Theory and research generally suggest that a leader, or one offender, directs the actions of another or others during these assaults. Some research suggests that violence is more common in such assaults. Research also suggests that young men in hypermasculine, limited-oversight contexts who have mental health issues or who are under the influence of substances may be more likely to engage in multiple-perpetrator sexual assault.

Conclusions and Implications for Prevention Efforts

While there is much more to learn about sexual assault perpetrators, several overarching themes emerge from this body of research that are relevant to the Air Force as it structures sexual assault prevention efforts.

1. Sexual Assault Perpetrators Are a Very Heterogeneous Group

Implication: To ensure that airmen as well as Air Force leaders are aware of the full range of possible perpetrator types, sexual assault prevention training should ensure that scenarios illustrate the heterogeneity of sexual assault perpetrators and include descriptions of the various known motivations, types, and offending patterns among perpetrators. This can help dispel any myths regarding how to identify a potential perpetrator.

2. Sexual Assault Perpetration Is Likely Influenced by Different Combinations of Factors

Implication: The complexity of factors influencing sexual assault perpetration and the multiple pathways that may lead an individual to commit a sexual assault make it difficult to predict whether an individual is likely to commit sexual assault. There are a number of factors, however, that research indicates are related to perpetration that may be susceptible to targeted-intervention efforts. Several studies demonstrate that certain attitudes and cognitions are associated with sexual assault perpetration by individuals, and that such attitudes may be changed through intervention. Because past perpetration of sexual assault is one of the most consistently found predictors of future sexual assault, the Air Force should continue screening out enlisted and officer recruits who have criminal histories of sexual assault. It should also explore additional mechanisms for identifying past perpetrators, including self-reported engagement in sexual assault. The Air Force should identify opportunities to address contextual or environmental factors, such as peer sexual aggression and the use of alcohol, that are associated with sexual assault perpetration. It should continue to target the full range of individuals serving in the Air

Force in establishing social norms that discourage sexual aggression and violence among incoming recruits and in emphasizing the importance of commanders' role in fostering a positive environment to prevent sexual assault.

3. Sexual Assault Perpetrators Make a Series of Decisions That Lead to Opportunities to Commit Assault

Implication: There may be decision points along the pathway to sexual assault when steps can be taken to prevent or intervene. For example, prevention efforts could target coping mechanisms to strengthen positive peer networks. Air Force efforts already under way may help decrease risk of sexual assault. For example, programs devoted to responsible alcohol consumption, including the Air Force's Alcohol and Drug Abuse Prevention and Treatment Program (ADAPT), bystander intervention programs, and social activities and facilities that are alternatives to bars may also disrupt decision points that could otherwise lead to sexual assault.

4. Very Little Is Known About Female, Male-on-Male, and Multiple-Perpetrator Sexual Assault Perpetrators

Implication: While there is not yet sufficient research evidence on these types of sexual assault perpetrators to point to any specific areas for developing prevention or intervention efforts, it is important for the Air Force to address these types of sexual assault as part of sexual assault awareness and prevention trainings. Addressing these types of assault will demonstrate to airmen that the Air Force considers all forms of sexual assault to be equally serious, and that the Air Force intends to detect and hold perpetrators accountable. This acknowledgment may prompt individuals who were victims of these types of assaults to report them, particularly if they did not think of themselves as victims of sexual assault or if they feared they would be not taken seriously by the Air Force.

Limitations and Future Research

There are several limitations to existing research on sexual assault. Most existing studies examine only one or a handful of factors potentially related to perpetration. Because we know sexual assault perpetration is likely influenced by a combination of factors, more comprehensive research is needed. Extant research literature also does not follow representative samples over time to understand how risk factors lead to sexual assault. Understanding how different factors interact over time and cause sexual assault will require longitudinal research designs that follow large cohorts of people over time. A deeper understanding of how and under what circumstances factors are associated with sexual assault will help determine where to focus prevention efforts.

Most existing studies examine characteristics and behaviors of perpetrators within the general population. Only a handful of studies have systematically explored the characteristics and behaviors of military personnel who commit sexual assault during their service. Much more research with Air Force populations is needed to understand whether the risk factors identified in other research generalize to the Air Force population and to identify whether there are additional contributors specific to the Air Force.

Acknowledgments

We are thankful to James Torr, who helped write the summary and provide overall editorial assistance. The report also benefited from the professional editing skills of Linda Theung and proofreading by Allison Kerns. We are also thankful to Andrew Morral, Coreen Farris, and Andra Tharp for their thoughtful comments and valuable feedback on earlier drafts of this report.

Abbreviations

CDC	Centers for Disease Control and Prevention
IRMA	Illinois Rape Myth Acceptance Scale
MMPI-2	Minnesota Multiphasic Personality Inventory-2
RMAS	Rape Myth Acceptance Scale
SID	seemingly irrelevant decision
WGRA	Workplace and Gender Relations Survey of Active Duty Members

1. Introduction

Sexual assault continues to be a pervasive problem in the United States. While prevalence estimates vary considerably based on research samples and definitions of sexual assault, a nationally representative survey estimates that 19.3 percent of women and 1.7 percent of men in the United States have been sexually assaulted at some point in their lifetime (Breiding et al., 2014). While we found only one study that makes direct comparisons between the prevalence of sexual assault in civilian and military populations (discussed below), several studies indicate that members of the military also experience high rates of sexual assault. Depending on the survey sample and definition used, military surveys have found that approximately 9 to 33 percent of female U.S. service members and 1 to 12 percent of male U.S. service members report experiencing attempted or completed sexual assault during their time in the military (Bostock and Daley, 2007; Murdoch et al., 2007; Hoyt, Rielage, and Williams, 2011). According to the 2012 Workplace and Gender Relations Survey of Active Duty Members (WGRA), which is administered by the Department of Defense and designed to assess the prevalence of sexual assault and sexual harassment across the entire active-duty force, an estimated 23 percent of female and 4 percent of male service members have been sexually assaulted during their military service (Rock, 2013).[2] A study by the Centers for Disease Control and Prevention (CDC) indicates that civilian and military service women face similar levels of risk for sexual assault (Black and Merrick, 2013).[3] We do not yet know how risk for assault compares between male civilians and members of the military.

The U.S. military has a vested interest in reducing military sexual assault, including preventing service members from perpetrating sexual assault against other service members or civilians. Sexual assault perpetrated by service members not only violates military law and values, it also decreases other service members' feelings of safety and well being, and it negatively impacts public perceptions of the U.S. Armed Forces and its service members. The Air Force recognizes the importance of drawing on existing empirical knowledge about sexual assault perpetration when shaping its ongoing efforts to combat sexual assault within the military. Some information about the characteristics of military sexual assault perpetrators and the circumstances surrounding these assaults can be gleaned through surveys such as the WGRA.

---

[2] In an effort to confirm or improve prevalence estimates for the military, the WGRA has undergone an expert review and revision. The 2014 sexual assault estimates from this revised survey are available in Morral et al., 2015.

[3] Active-duty women who were deployed during the three years prior to the survey are an exception. Those women were significantly more likely to experience intimate-partner violence and contact sexual violence compared with active-duty women not deployed. There are also differences in type of perpetrator across populations. For example, smaller proportions of active-duty women and wives of active-duty men experienced lifetime physical violence, rape, or stalking by an intimate partner.

There is still much that is not known, however, about these groups of offenders, including historical and personality individual risk factors for committing sexual assault in the military and actions surrounding these assaults (Turchik and Wilson, 2010). With these issues in mind, we sought to provide the Air Force with a better understanding of sexual assault perpetrator risk factors and behaviors to help inform sexual assault prevention and training efforts. This report presents our findings from a review of literature on the characteristics and behaviors of sexual assault perpetration.

The primary objective of this report is educational in nature—to inform the Air Force about what is empirically known about sexual assault perpetrator risk factors and behaviors. After synthesizing this body of literature, our second aim is to highlight important findings within the literature that could guide ongoing and future Air Force sexual assault prevention and training efforts. Finally, at the Air Force's request, we searched the literature for any tools to predict sexual assault perpetration that could potentially be incorporated into the recruitment screening of airmen. We also address the applicability of incorporating empirically identified risk factors into an Air Force screening tool in the conclusion of this report.

While very limited information exists about military sexual assault perpetrator risk factors, since the 1970s a growing body of research has been devoted to understanding sexual assault within the general population. A good number of these studies have considered the etiology of sexual assault perpetration and the behavior of those individuals who commit sexual assault. We therefore reviewed both civilian and military population studies to provide a deeper understanding of why individuals commit sexual assault, the characteristics most frequently associated with sexual assault perpetrators, and common patterns of behavior among this group of offenders. While we conclude this report with a discussion of the literature's implications for prevention and training efforts, it was beyond the scope of this report to conduct a full review of the empirical literature on sexual assault–prevention programs. Rather, we refer to this literature in our discussion and direct interested readers to recent meta-analyses (i.e., statistical summaries that integrate results across many individual studies) and summaries of this body of research.

Methodology

We conducted a review of existing literature on the characteristics and behaviors of adults who commit sexual assault against other adults. We began by conducting searches for empirical journal articles on social/behavioral-science search engines (e.g., PsycINFO, Web of Science) using specific search terms, such as *sexual assault perpetration*, *sexual aggression*, and *rape*. To provide the Air Force with a picture of the most current knowledge about the characteristics and behaviors of sexual assault perpetrators, we conducted our search by examining empirical literature and books on sexual offending published from the years 2000 to 2014. We supplemented the recent literature with pre-2000 research related to these topics. We next conducted a snowball-sampling approach by scanning literature identified during the online search and flagging additional referenced articles for inclusion in our review. In total, we identified more than 150 relevant articles and books.

For the purposes of this report, we considered research examining a broad spectrum of behaviors related to sexual assault. Researchers have used a number of different terms, including *sexual coercion, sexual aggression, sexual assault, sexual offending, rape*, and *sexual assault perpetration* when studying individuals who perform unwanted sexual behaviors against another person (Lyndon, White, and Kadlec, 2007). Furthermore, definitions of specific terms have varied between studies. For example, some studies have limited examinations of sexual coercion to instances of verbal or emotional pressure (e.g., Testa and Dermen, 1999), whereas others have defined sexual coercion more broadly to include verbal force, physical force, or other methods of incapacitation (e.g., alcohol and drugs) to obtain sexual gratification (e.g., Adams-Curtis and Forbes, 2004). To account for these variations, our review considered the wide range of terms and associated behaviors studied within this body of literature. Throughout this report, the term *sexual assault perpetration* refers to the broad range of behaviors and tactics committed by perpetrators (i.e., physical, psychological, or verbal threats, and other methods of incapacitation) to perform an unwanted sexual act against another person. Unwanted sexual acts range from sexual contact to oral, anal, or vaginal intercourse. We also considered the range of possible relationships between perpetrators and victims, including strangers, acquaintances, intimate partners/spouses,[4] and groups of perpetrators who commit sexual assault against strangers or known victims.

Finally, while sexual assault perpetration is most commonly conceptualized as a situation in which a man commits sexual assault against a woman, both men and women can perpetrate and be victims of sexual assault. Therefore, while the majority of existing research has focused on male perpetrators who assault female victims, we also made an effort to search specifically for research on other types of perpetrators—female sexual assault perpetrators, men who perpetrate assault against other men, and perpetrators who participate in group sexual assault.

Limitations of Existing Research on Sexual Assault Perpetration

While an extensive literature on sexual assault perpetration has been produced in the past 40 years, researchers have noted some limitations to existing research (e.g., Abbey, 2011). There is still much that can be learned from the plethora of studies that have begun to explore sexual assault perpetration, but it is important to acknowledge some of the most commonly cited limitations to this body of research and discuss their implications for what we are able to conclude from these lines of research.

---

[4] We included studies on intimate partner/spousal rape, but we did not delve into the literature on domestic violence because it was beyond the scope of this review.

To gather knowledge about the characteristics and behaviors of sexual assault perpetrators, most empirical research has relied on one of two strategies or approaches. One approach involves studying offenders who are or have been adjudicated for sexual assault. Researchers most often gather information about these convicted sex offenders though surveys/interviews with the offenders or through archival analyses of case information or police reports. When comparison groups are included in the study designs, adjudicated sexual assault offenders are typically compared with other groups of adjudicated offenders—for example, adult sexual assault perpetrators are compared with child molesters or sexual assault offenders are compared with nonsexual, violent offenders. Research with adjudicated samples, therefore, gathers information about a specific type of offender—those individuals whose crimes are reported and who are identified, arrested, and convicted of their crime. Research indicates, however, that most sexual assaults are not reported to the police. Furthermore, victims of stranger assaults, victims who are assaulted with a weapon or other means of force, and victims who felt that their life was in danger are more likely to formally provide a report than victims who are assaulted by someone they know (Bachman, 1998; Feldhaus, Houry, and Kaminsky, 2000; Felson, Messner, and Hoskin, 1999; Fisher and Walters, 2003; Gartner and Macmillan, 1995; Pino and Meier, 1999). Therefore, studies with adjudicated samples represent a very specific subset of sexual assault perpetrators.

Another approach is to draw samples from community members (i.e., individuals from the general population) or from college students in an effort to include sexual assault that may not be reported to the criminal-justice system. These studies commonly survey participants about their prior sexual experiences, as well as one or more characteristics hypothesized to be related to sexual assault perpetration—for example, experiences with childhood abuse or attitudes toward women. The characteristics of individuals who admit to committing some form of sexual assault are compared with those who do not admit to perpetrating sexual assault.

While both approaches have provided valuable information about sexual assault perpetration, there are some limitations to these lines of research. First, both of these approaches commonly rely on surveys or interviews in which participants supply retrospective self-reports about their past experiences. Participants may feel uncomfortable reporting some of these sensitive experiences, or they may not accurately remember the past—for example, instances of childhood abuse or age of first sexual experience. In addition, adjudicated samples may have particular motivations to lie about their past. While most studies ask participants to report past experiences, there are a small number of longitudinal studies that follow cohorts of participants over a period of time. Longitudinal designs provide insight into the developmental pathways or trajectories that may lead to sexual assault perpetration, but more longitudinal studies are needed before we have a clear understanding of the developmental pathways leading to sexual assault perpetration.

Second, studies have varied definitions of sexual assault perpetration. Some studies have defined sexual assault perpetration very broadly to include sexually aggressive behavior and verbal coercion, while other studies have limited the scope of exploration only to acts that would meet the legal definition of sexual assault/rape. Differences in sexual assault definitions make cross-study comparisons challenging, particularly when some studies find effects of a particular factor, while other studies fail to find an effect. In these situations, we do not know whether the differences are due to variations in the ways that sexual assault is defined or to other factors.

Third, as will be demonstrated in this report, sexual assault perpetration is a complex issue, likely influenced by a variety of factors—including developmental, biological, psychological, and sociological factors—that may interact in a number of different ways across different people (Terry, 2012). Most existing sexual assault perpetration studies, however, have examined only one or a small number of factors. While these studies have individually identified a number of factors that are associated with sexual assault perpetration, it is still unclear how these factors interact to influence sexual assault perpetration. In addition, some factors have predominantly been studied in either college students or adjudicated populations. In these cases, we do not know whether a factor found to be correlated with sexual assault perpetration in a college-student population is also correlated with sexual assault perpetration in adjudicated populations.

Finally, the vast majority of existing research has focused on male perpetrators who assault female victims. This focus is perhaps justified, in that studies measuring the frequency of perpetration indicate that sexual assault is largely committed by men against female victims (Tjaden and Thoennes, 2006). Research does also indicate, however, that a proportion of both civilian and military men have experienced attempted rape or completed rape (Black et al., 2011; Rock, 2013). It is therefore important to understand the characteristics and behaviors of those individuals who perpetrate sexual assault against men. In recent years, lines of research have also begun to explore the characteristics and behaviors of female sexual assault perpetrators, men who assault other men, and individuals who perpetrate sexual assault in groups. To date, however, we know significantly less about the characteristics of these types of perpetrators compared with male perpetrators who assault female victims.

Despite these limitations, the body of literature as a whole still provides valuable information about the characteristics and behaviors of sexual assault perpetrators, particularly male perpetrators who assault female victims. While there is still more research to be done, these studies have provided a rich amount of information that is important to consider when developing responses to prevent sexual assault.

Organization of the Report

The remaining chapters in this report provide an overview of the recent empirical literature on the characteristics and behaviors of adults who commit sexual assault against other adults. Chapters Two and Three focus specifically on male perpetrators who sexually assault female victims, since this represents the majority of empirical research. Chapter Two provides a summary of the characteristics that have been most commonly identified by empirical research for male perpetrators who assault female victims. Chapter Three discusses the common behaviors of male perpetrators who assault female victims. Chapters Four through Six then provide a summary of empirical literature on other types of offenders. Chapter Four provides a summary of the limited existing literature on women who commit sexual assault, including typologies of female sexual offenders and their characteristics and offending behavioral patterns. Chapter Five reviews the limited studies on male perpetrators who sexually assault other men, including existing typologies of male-male sexual assault perpetrators and their characteristics and behaviors. Chapter Six provides an overview of the existing literature on group sexual assault perpetration. Finally, based on this review, Chapter Seven provides conclusions and implications for prevention, training, and recruitment to help the Air Force in its efforts to combat sexual assault among service members.

2. Characteristics of Male Perpetrators Who Sexually Assault Female Victims

A significant body of research has been devoted to examining the common characteristics of male perpetrators who sexually assault female victims. A deeper understanding of the characteristics most frequently associated with sexual assault perpetrators is useful in understanding the etiology of sexual assault perpetration and may be useful for identifying possible methods of intervention and prevention. Within the past 40 years, researchers have examined a wide array of characteristics potentially related to sexual assault perpetration. In this chapter, we describe the most commonly studied factors that have been found to be associated with sexual assault perpetration. In general, these characteristics can be grouped into several broad categories: historical/developmental factors, including childhood abuse and sexual behavior; individual characteristics, including interpersonal skills and cognitions; and contextual factors, including perceptions of peer attitudes/behavior and alcohol/drug use (Tharp et al., 2013). While other recent research (e.g., Jewkes, 2012, and Tharp et al., 2013) has conducted reviews of the literature on sexual assault perpetration, our review differs slightly in that it primarily focuses on studies examining adult sexual assault perpetrators, although particularly with college samples, some teenagers under the age of 18 may be included. In addition, with a few exceptions, we mostly focused on research drawing from U.S. samples; in certain cases, we included international sample studies either because they were frequently cited in the perpetration literature (e.g., Senn et al., 2000) or because they supplemented the sparse U.S. literature on a particular factor (e.g., drug use). Finally, given the purpose of this report to provide guidance to the Air Force in prevention and recruitment efforts, we mostly focused this review on factors that have been studied at least several times within the recent literature (i.e., 2000 or later). We did, however, make an effort to review other factors that were commonly mentioned as potential risk factors in earlier literature. It should be noted that while research has identified a broad range of factors associated with sexual assault perpetration, no single factor has been found to be highly predictive of committing sexual assault. Rather, researchers agree that myriad factors likely interact to lead to sexual assault perpetration, the exact combination of which likely varies among perpetrators (Abbey et al., 2001; Terry, 2012; Tharp et al., 2013). Table 3.1 provides an overview of commonly studied characteristics identified in our literature review.

Table 3.1. Characteristics of Male Perpetrators Who Sexually Assault Female Victims

Factor	Summary of Literature
Childhood abuse	
Childhood sexual abuse	Many studies that found an effect have included child molesters in the sample. It may be that childhood sexual abuse does not play as strong of a role in adult sexual assault perpetration.
Childhood physical abuse	Several studies with adjudicated offenders have found higher rates of child physical abuse in adult sexual assault perpetrators compared with other groups of offenders; a few studies did not find an effect.
Childhood emotional abuse	A handful of studies have found an association between childhood emotional abuse and sexual assault perpetration in both adjudicated and college samples. One study indicates that the relationship may be mediated by hostile attitudes toward women.
Exposure to family violence	Less existing research, but several studies with college-student samples, have found associations between parental conflict and sexual assault perpetration as an adolescent or adult.
Sexual behavior	
Multiple sex partners and early initiation of sex	A number of surveys with college students and with members of the community have found a correlation between multiple sexual partners and/or early initiation of sex and self-reported sexual assault perpetration. Some studies have examined the relationship between multiple sex partners and early initiation of sex separately, while many other studies have combined the variables to create a "promiscuity score."
Casual attitudes toward sex	Several studies have found a link between sexual assault perpetration and beliefs that sex outside of a relationship is acceptable. Casual attitudes toward sex were also found to interact with hypermasculinity to predict sexual assault perpetration.
Past sexual violence perpetration	A number of studies, both prospective and retrospective, have found an association with sexual assault perpetration.
Interpersonal skills	
Social-skill deficits	Some studies have found adjudicated offenders report more difficulties in social skill; a number of studies found no effect. Social-skill deficits may be more likely in child molesters compared with adult sexual assault perpetrators.
Lack of empathy	Results seem to differ based on type of empathy measured; more studies find effects when measuring sexual assault victim-specific empathy.
Attachment styles	A handful of studies thus far provide some support for an association between attachment styles and adult sexual assault perpetration.
Sex misinterpretation	Several college and community studies found a link with misinterpretation of cues from women as sexual invitations. This was also found to be moderated by alcohol use; one study failed to find an effect.
Attitudes and cognitions	
Hostility toward women	Many studies with college and community samples found an association; some studies have failed to find an effect.

Factor	Summary of Literature
Rape myth acceptance	Many studies have found an association; a few studies have not. Newer scales have been developed to respond to criticisms of original measures, but not as extensively tested. A recent meta-analysis found a strong relationship between scores on the rape myth–acceptance scale and sexual assault perpetration.
Belief in traditional gender roles	Several college and community studies found an association with beliefs in traditional gender roles.
Hypermasculinity	Several studies found an association between endorsements of masculine traits and measures of hypermasculinity. A meta-analysis found hypermasculinity to be moderately related to sexual aggression.
Peer attitudes and behavior	
Perceptions of peer's sexual attitudes and behavior	Several college sample studies have found sexual assault perpetration to be more likely for those who associate with peers who are perceived to be sexually aggressive. Several college studies, both retrospective and prospective, have found a sexual assault perpetration association with perceptions that peers endorse sexual assault.
Substance use	
Alcohol use	There is consistent agreement that alcohol use is associated with sexual assault perpetration. This has mostly been studied in college populations.
Drug use	A limited number of studies have produced mixed findings, with some studies finding effects for some drugs, but not other drugs, and other studies failing to find an association.

Childhood Abuse

Childhood abuse—sexual abuse, physical abuse, emotional abuse, and exposure to violence within the home—has often been purported to be related to sexual assault perpetration later as an adult. The exploration of an association between childhood abuse and sexual assault perpetration later in adulthood is driven by research indicating a link between childhood abuse and later problems in adulthood, such as functioning in adult interpersonal relationships, substance abuse, depression, suicide, and various forms of violent behavior (e.g., Tyler, 2002, and Widom, 2001). While research has identified a high incidence of childhood abuse in adult sexual assault perpetrators (Simons, Wurtele, and Heil, 2002), the research specifically examining a link between childhood abuse and sexual assault perpetration has produced mixed results. In addition, a good number of studies have collapsed across forms of child abuse and/or various forms of sexual assault perpetration (e.g., adult rape, child molestation), making it difficult to distinguish the exact influence of particular forms of childhood abuse on different types of sexual assault perpetration. Below, we provide more details on lines of research examining links between sexual assault perpetration and various forms of child abuse.

Childhood Sexual Abuse

Victim-to-victimizer theory purports that exposure to sexual abuse as a child leads the victim to reenact that childhood trauma as an adult on victims of his or her own (Hanson and Slater, 1988; Simons, Wurtele, and Heil, 2002). Interviews and surveys of men incarcerated for various forms of sexual assault have found that a high number, between 25 and 70 percent, self-report having been abused as a child (Simons, Wurtele, and Heil, 2002). Studies comparing rates of childhood sexual abuse in sexual assault perpetrators with other groups, however, have produced mixed findings, with some studies finding some support for an association (Abbey et al., 2006, and Knight and Sims-Knight, 2003), and others failing to find that adult sexual assault perpetrators were more likely to report childhood sexual abuse than comparison groups (McCormack, Hudson, and Ward, 2002). Some researchers have hypothesized that these differences in findings may be due to differences in samples across studies. Specifically, studies that examined both child molesters and adult rapists more frequently identified an association between childhood sexual assault and later sexual assault perpetration, while studies that limited their sample to perpetrators of adult sexual assault often failed to find an effect. Results of a meta-analysis suggested that sexual offenders against adults are more likely than sex offenders against children to have suffered child physical abuse, and sexual offenders against children are more likely than sex offenders against adults to have been sexually abused as children (Jespersen, Lalumière, and Seto, 2009). Other research has examined the role of empathy in the relationship between childhood sexual and physical abuse and sexual assault perpetration (Simons, Wurtele, and Heil, 2002). Researchers have hypothesized that the traumatic experiences of childhood abuse and the associated lack of humane treatment decreases the ability to empathize with others as adults (Bandura, Underwood, and Fromson, 1975). Bolstering researchers' hypothesis that child sexual abuse more strongly predicts childhood molestation, in one study, childhood sexual abuse did not predict perpetration of assault against adult victims; rather, offenders who reported childhood sexual abuse and childhood exposure to pornography were less empathetic to child victims and reported perpetrating sexual abuse toward more child victims (Simons, Wurtele, and Heil, 2002).

Most of the studies examining a link between childhood sexual abuse and adult sexual assault perpetration have relied on retrospective self-reports, most often with incarcerated individuals who may have motivations to lie about their past experiences. Incarcerated sexual assault perpetrators are also likely to possess different characteristics from non-incarcerated offenders. For example, incarcerated sexual assault perpetrators were more likely than non-incarcerated sexual assault perpetrators to have assaulted strangers and/or used a weapon during the offense (Bachman, 1998, and Feldhaus, Houry, and Kaminsky, 2000). Therefore it is difficult to generalize research findings with incarcerated samples to the majority of offenders who have not been incarcerated for their assaults.

One study attempted to improve on past research designs by conducting a prospective study with undergraduate college students (Loh and Gidycz, 2005). In this study, 325 college men completed baseline measures, including measures of childhood sexual assault and sexually aggressive behavior during adolescence. To prospectively study this issue, researchers again gathered measures of sexually aggressive behavior three months after collecting baseline measures. At baseline, they found that individuals who experienced sexual assault as a child were six times more likely to also have a history of engaging in sexually aggressive behavior. When included in a model to explain sexual assault aggression, however, only 5 percent of the sexual aggression was explained by previous sexual victimization as a child. When conducting the prospective analysis, childhood sexual victimization did not predict later engagement in sexually aggressive behavior. The only factor that reliably predicted engaging in sexually aggressive acts three months later was having a history of sexual assault perpetration: Individuals with such a history were nine times more likely to engage in sexually aggressive behavior during the three-month period.

Childhood Physical Abuse

Several studies have established a link between physical abuse during childhood and later engagement in a variety of violent and aggressive behavior as an adult (Muller and Diamond, 1999, and Widom and Shepard, 1996). Researchers have posited that subjection to physical violence as a child establishes a pattern of violence in interpersonal relationships. Researchers have hypothesized that these experiences in early childhood may instill sexual interests that involve coercion or force (Lee et al., 2002, and Simons, Wurtele, and Heil, 2002). Research examining childhood physical abuse has found that boys subjected to physical violence in the home are more likely to later be arrested for a violent sex crime (Widom and Ames, 1994). Other research has found sexual assault perpetrators to be more likely to have experiences of childhood physical abuse than nonviolent offenders (Lee et al., 2002). One study failed to find an association between childhood physical abuse and adult sexual assault perpetration (McCormack, Hudson, and Ward, 2002).

While studies have found that a high number of sexual assault perpetrators report experiencing abuse as a child, obviously not all children subjected to violence grow up to become sexual assault perpetrators. Therefore, some recent research has focused on identifying variables that mediate, or explain, the relationship between childhood abuse and adult sexual assault perpetration. For example, research has examined the role of empathy in the relationship between childhood sexual and physical abuse and sexual assault perpetration (Simons, Wurtele, and Heil, 2002). Researchers have hypothesized that the traumatic experiences of childhood abuse and the associated lack of humane treatment decreases victims' ability to empathize with others as adults (Bandura, Underwood, and Fromson, 1975). They found that incarcerated offenders who self-reported childhood physical abuse were less empathetic to female victims and reported perpetrating sexual assault against more adult victims.

Childhood Emotional Abuse

In recent years, researchers have begun examining the link between childhood emotional abuse and later sexual assault perpetration. According to the CDC, childhood emotional abuse can include behaviors "that harm a child's self-worth or emotional well-being such as name-calling, shaming, rejection, withholding love, or threats" (Leeb et al., 2008). Exposure to childhood emotional abuse appears to have deleterious effects, including negative emotions, such as anger and irritability (Teicher et al., 2006), and difficulties in adult relationships (Davis, Petretic-Jackson, and Ting, 2001, and Perry, DiLillo, and Peugh, 2007). Thus, researchers have hypothesized that childhood emotional abuse may be associated with later sexual assault perpetration. While still limited in number, studies have found an association between childhood emotional abuse and sexual assault perpetration as an adult. Research has found that, compared with nonsexual offenders, sexual assault perpetrators are more likely to report childhood emotional abuse. Research controlling for other forms of childhood abuse has found childhood emotional abuse to be associated with physically forced sexual assault perpetration in both college-student samples and adjudicated samples (DeGue and DiLillo, 2005, and DeGue, DiLillo, and Scalora, 2010).

Other research exploring factors that might explain the relationship between childhood emotional abuse and sexual assault perpetration has found that expressing hostile attitudes toward women mediated the relationship between childhood emotional abuse and later sexual assault perpetration in an adjudicated sample of offenders (Vivolo-Kantor et al., 2013). This particular sample of adjudicated offenders included both individuals who had committed sexual assault against adults and against children. The results of these findings may indicate that, when experiencing childhood emotional abuse at the hands of caregivers leads to hostility toward women, there may be an increase in the likelihood of perpetrating sexual assault as an adult.

Childhood Exposure to Family Violence

Research has found that, in addition to subjection to childhood abuse, exposure to family violence is also associated with youth violence (Widom, 2001) and violence as an adult (Kaufman and Zigler, 1987). Expanding on the idea that exposure to family violence during childhood provides models for interpersonal relationships in adulthood, a limited number of studies have explored the relationship between childhood exposure to family violence and later sexual assault perpetration.

One study of college freshmen found that witnessing domestic violence during childhood was predictive of committing both sexual and physical assault against an intimate partner (White et al., 2008). Another study examining the role of childhood exposure to violence followed incoming college freshmen over the course of five years (White and Smith, 2004). In the first year of the study, participants were asked to report historical information, including sexual assault perpetration during adolescence and exposure to family violence during childhood. The study found that witnessing violence during childhood was predictive of sexual assault perpetration in high school. No forms of child maltreatment, including witnessing violence, however, were predictive of sexual assault perpetration in college after controlling for sexual assault perpetration in high school. The researchers conclude that childhood victimization, including witnessing violence in the home, and sexual assault perpetration during adolescence may be precursors to sexual violence as young adults, with the effects of exposure to family violence indirectly affecting sexual assault perpetration by having an effect on adolescent behavior.

Conclusion

While at least some research seems to indicate a relationship between childhood sexual abuse and later sexual assault perpetration, findings are mixed, and more research is needed to fully explore the mechanisms of this relationship and the conditions in which this relationship occurs. The link between physical childhood abuse and exposure to family violence appears to be more established, although more research is needed to understand how those factors explain the relationship between childhood abuse and later sexual assault perpetration.

Prior Sexual Behavior

Another line of research has established a link between individuals' prior sexual behavior and the likelihood of adult sexual aggression. Below, we describe some of the most frequently studied sexual behaviors, including number of sex partners, early initiation of sex, impersonal or casual attitudes toward sex, and past sexual violence perpetration.

Multiple Partners and Early Initiation of Sex

A number of surveys with college students and with members of the community at large found a correlation between multiple sexual partners and/or early initiation of sex and self-reported perpetration of sexual violence (Abbey and McAuslan, 2004; Hall et al., 2005; Merrill et al., 2001; Parkhill and Abbey, 2008; Senn et al., 2000). Researchers have hypothesized that these factors may be related to sexual assault perpetration because these individuals have a high degree of interest in sex and because the frequency of sexual experiences provides more opportunities to engage in sexually coercive behaviors (Kanin, 1985, and Malamuth et al., 1991).

Some studies have examined the relationship between multiple sex partners and early initiation of sex separately, while many other studies have created a "promiscuity score" based on respondents' answers to questions related to each variable. For example, one study of 195 Canadian men created a promiscuity score based on men's answers to questions about the age at which they started their first sexual relationship and questions related to their number of sexual/romantic partners. They found that respondents' promiscuity scores significantly predicted self-reported sexual coercion (Senn et al., 2000). In other research, measures of promiscuity, constructed from the age of first sexual relationship and lifetime number of sexual partners, were found to be predictive of sexual aggression (Malamuth et al., 1991 and 1995). Another study found that number of sexual partners mediated, or partially explained, the relationship between childhood sexual abuse and later perpetration of sexual assault in a sample of Navy recruits (Merrill et al., 2001).

Casual Attitudes Toward Sex

Studies have also identified a significant link between impersonal attitudes toward sex (defined as practices and beliefs that sex outside a relationship is acceptable) and sexual assault perpetration. According to researchers, men with impersonal attitudes toward sex prefer casual sexual encounters to committed relationships and are motivated to have sex for sexual gratification rather than to feel intimacy or emotional closeness (Malamuth et al., 1991). A casual attitude toward sex is also likely related to having multiple partners, therefore providing more opportunities to use coercive tactics to obtain sex.

Researchers found that college students and community members with impersonal attitudes toward sex—indicated, for example, by endorsing statements such as "sex without love is OK"—are more likely to admit to commit sexual assault perpetration (Abbey et al., 2006; Abbey et al., 2007; White et al., 2008; Zawacki et al., 2003). For example, one study gathering self-reports from a sample of community men found that casual attitudes toward sex were directly related to the number of sexual assaults committed (Abbey et al., 2006). In addition, the data indicated that the more alcohol-abuse issues these men reported, the more likely they were to report casual attitudes toward sex (Abbey et al., 2006).

Past Sexual Violence Perpetration

Finally, a number of studies with college students and community members have consistently found a history of sexual assault perpetration to be associated or predictive of additional sexual assault perpetration (Gidycz et al., 2007; Hall et al., 2005; Loh and Gidycz, 2006; Loh et al., 2005; Malamuth, 1995; White and Smith, 2004). This finding is not particularly surprising, considering that researchers have estimated the recidivism rate for sexual assault perpetration to be between 14 and 68 percent (Hanson and Morton-Bourgon, 2005, and Zinzow and Thompson, 2014). These estimates likely vary based on the samples used (i.e., incarcerated samples versus college students) and the measurements used (i.e., law enforcement data versus self-reports on a wide range of sexually aggressive behaviors).

For example, one study of 325 college-age men measured sexual assault perpetration three times over the course of seven months—at pretest, three-month follow-up, and seven-month follow-up—and found that perpetration of sexual assault at any assessment period was predictive of sexual assault perpetration during the subsequent assessment period (Loh et al., 2005). In another case, researchers conducted a ten-year follow-up study on participants used to develop the Confluence Model of sexual aggression (Malamuth et al., 1991). They found that their earlier offenses were predictive of additional sexual aggression, and that sexually aggressive men are likely to offend multiple times (Malamuth et al., 1995). Another study followed incoming college freshmen over the course of five years and found that self-reports of committing sexual assault in high school were predictive of perpetrating sexual assault during college; 24 percent of the variance in predicting incidents of sexual assault perpetration in college could be attributed to sexual assault committed during high school (White and Smith, 2004).

Conclusion

Various aspects of an individual's past sexual behavior have been found to be associated with later sexual assault perpetration. Not surprisingly, one of the most consistently identified sexual behaviors is whether a person has committed sexual assault in the past. Some research has found other sexual behaviors related to an individual's level of promiscuity and casualness toward sexual relations to be linked to increased likelihood of perpetrating sexual assault. It is important to note, however, that many of these studies (e.g., Malamuth, 1995) found past sexual behavior to be just one component, and other factors (such as family dysfunction or association with delinquent peers) interacted with prior sexual behavior to increase the likelihood of sexual assault perpetration.

Interpersonal Skills

A number of studies have examined whether sexual assault perpetrators are likely to display deficits in their interpersonal skills—including social-skill deficits, empathetic deficits, and intimacy/attachment issues in their personal relationships. These areas of study are rooted in psychological-attachment theories, which posit that during developmental years, individuals develop bonds that provide the foundation for pro-social, intimate relationships as adults (Marshall and Barbaree, 1990). According to attachment theory, when this foundation is absent, individuals may try to experience intimacy inappropriately. Below, we describe some of the most frequently studied factors found to be associated with sexual assault perpetration.

Social-Skill Deficits

A long-held theory within the sexual assault perpetration literature is that individuals may perpetrate sexual assault to achieve sexual gratification to compensate for difficulties they experience interacting with members of the opposite sex (Geer, Estupinan, and Manguno-Mire, 2000). Some studies using adjudicated samples have found that incarcerated sexual assault perpetrators were more likely to display some skill deficits in comparison with non–sex offenders, for example, on measures of extroversion and physiological arousal during role-play activities (Gudjonsson and Sigurdsson, 2000, and Overholser and Beck, 1986). A number of studies, however, have failed to find an effect of social-skill deficits on sexual assault perpetration (e.g., Fernandez and Marshall, 2003, and Grier, 1988). The dearth of research over time that has failed to find a relationship between social skill and sexual assault perpetration has led a number of researchers to conclude that social skill do not play a significant role in adult sexual assault perpetration (McFall, 1990). Other researchers have hypothesized that social-skill deficits may be more prevalent among child molesters than among adult sexual assault perpetrators (Geer, Estupinan, and Manguno-Mire, 2000).

Empathy Deficits

Researchers have hypothesized that sexual assault perpetrators lack empathy, or the ability to relate to someone else's feelings (Marshall et al., 1995). Studies examining a link between empathic deficits and sexual assault perpetration have produced different results, depending on the type of empathy measured. Some studies measuring generalized empathy have failed to find significant differences in empathic levels between sexual assault perpetrators and comparison groups (Langevin, Wright, and Handy, 1988, and Marshall et al., 1995). Other studies measuring empathy specifically related to victims of sexual assault, however, have found that sexual assault perpetrators exhibit lower levels of empathy toward victims of sexual assault than non-offenders (McGrath, Cann, and Konopasky, 1998, and Rice et al., 1994). Another recent study found that generalized empathy scores moderated the relationship between hostility toward women and sexual aggression, such that men who scored low on ratings of general empathy toward others and high on rating of hostility toward women and impersonal sex were more likely to be sexually aggressive compared with other men in the study (Wheeler, George, and Dahl, 2002). In a discussion of their findings, the researchers hypothesized that generalized empathy may need to interact with other variables, in this case impersonal sex and hostility toward women, to play a role in explaining sexual aggression (Wheeler, George, and Dahl, 2002).

Attachment

Some research has explored the relationship between attachment and sexual assault perpetration. This line of research draws from attachment theories, which assert the necessity of forming emotional bonds to others during the formative years, particularly during adolescence (Marshall and Barbaree, 1990). According to attachment theory, if these bonds are not formed, individuals develop insecure attachment styles. Sexual assault researchers have posited that individuals with insecure attachments to others fail to develop necessary components for intimate adult relationships (for example, interpersonal skills and self-confidence), which in turn can lead to sexual aggression (Ward et al., 1995). A handful of studies thus far have empirically explored the relationship between attachment and sexual assault perpetration and provide some support for an association between attachment styles and adult sexual assault perpetration (Abbey et al., 2007; Lyn and Burton, 2005; Smallbone and Dadds, 2000). For example, one study surveyed 162 Australian male college students about attachment during childhood, adult attachment, and maladaptive behaviors, such as anti-socialness, aggression, and coercive sexual behavior (Smallbone and Dadds, 2000). After controlling for anti-socialness and aggression, childhood-attachment scores predicted adult sexual assault perpetration. Another study interviewing a community sample of African and Caucasian men about a variety of factors thought to be associated with sexual assault perpetration found a relationship between lower scores on an adult-attachment scale and sexual assault perpetration (Abbey et al., 2007). One study examined attachment styles of child molesters; adult sexual assault perpetrators; violent nonsexual offenders; and nonviolent, non–sex offenders (Ward et al., 1995) and found that, while adult sexual assault perpetrators were more likely to be insecurely attached, so were all of the other offender groups.

Sexual Misinterpretation

Research on male expectancies indicates that sexually aggressive men are more likely than nonaggressive men to misperceive a woman's friendliness as a sign of sexual interest (Abbey and McAuslan, 2004; Abbey et al., 2001; Abbey, 2002). Researchers have hypothesized that there are several pathways in which sexual misinterpretation could lead to sexual assault perpetration (Farris et al., 2008a). For example, a man who misinterprets initial interactions with a woman as indicative of sexual interest may feel led on at the point when a woman's actual disinterest becomes clear, which leads him to become angry and violent. Alternatively, it may be the case that misinterpretation of sexual interest is a general difficulty in the interpretation of nonverbal cues from others.

Whatever the pathway, some studies using college-student samples have found an association between misinterpretation of sexual cues and sexual assault perpetration (Abbey and McAuslan, 2004; Abbey, McAuslan, and Ross, 1998; Yescavage, 1999). Other research indicates that sex misinterpretation may be associated with other factors. These studies have found that endorsing rape-supportive attitudes (Farris et al., 2008b) and consuming alcohol (Zawacki et al., 2003) are associated with sexual misperception.

Conclusion

There is at least some research indicating that sexual assault perpetrators may show differences in attachment styles, have lower empathy toward sexual assault victims, and misinterpret sexual cues. Some research with incarcerated samples indicates that sexual assault perpetrators may display deficits in social skill, but a number of studies have failed to find an effect in samples that include child molesters, calling into question the relationship between social skill and adult sexual assault perpetration. Research examining a link between interpersonal skills and sexual assault perpetration is somewhat mixed. More research is needed to clarify the mechanisms through which these interpersonal deficits have an effect and the role that other factors play in exacerbating difficulties in interpersonal skills.

Gender-Related Attitudes and Cognitions

Research has found a number of gender-related attitudes and cognitions related to an increased likelihood of committing sexual assault, including negative thoughts and attitudes toward women, ideologies about gender roles and masculinity, and misperceptions about women's role in sexual assault. The role of gender-related attitudes and cognitions has been among the most-studied factors in the sexual assault perpetration research, in part because rape is often conceptualized as an expression of anger against women or a method of obtaining dominance and control over women. Below, we summarize the research examining the role of gender-related cognitions and attitudes in sexual assault perpetration.

Hostility Toward Women

Some research has examined whether men who express hostile attitudes toward women are more likely to commit sexual assault. Hostility toward women is typically measured though the Hostility Toward Women scale, which assesses angry and distrustful attitudes toward women (e.g., "It is safer not to trust women") (Check, 1985). A number of studies have found an association between high Hostility Toward Women scores and sexual assault perpetration (Abbey et al., 2001; Abbey and McAuslan, 2004; Carr and VanDeusen, 2004; DeGue and DiLillo, 2005; DeGue, DiLillo, and Scalora, 2010; Forbes, Adams-Curtis, and White, 2004; Loh et al., 2005; Parkhill and Abbey, 2008; Smith and Stewart, 2003; Vega and Malamuth, 2007). Other research, however, has produced mixed or null results on the effects of hostility toward women (Abbey et al., 2007; Calhoun et al., 1997; Hall et al., 2005; Ménard et al., 2003).

Yet, other research has found significant effects only when hostility toward women interacted with other factors. One study with a sample of Asian American men found that using alcohol before or during sexual intercourse mediated the relationship between hostile attitudes toward women and sexual aggression (Hall et al., 2000). In a second study with a sample of European American men, however, alcohol did not mediate the relationship between hostility toward men and sexual aggression (Hall et al., 2000). Other research found that empathy moderated the relationship between hostility toward women and sexual aggression, such that men who scored low on ratings of general empathy toward others and high on rating of hostility toward women and impersonal sex were more likely to be sexually aggressive compared with other men in the study (Wheeler, George, and Dahl, 2002). Finally, other research exploring factors that might explain the relationship between childhood emotional abuse and sexual assault perpetration found that expressing hostile attitudes toward women mediated or explained the relationship between childhood emotional abuse and later sexual assault perpetration in an adjudicated sample of offenders (Vivolo-Kantor et al., 2013).

Rape Myth Acceptance

A number of studies have examined links between sexual assault perpetration and the endorsement of rape myths. Rape myths are defined as commonly held misperceptions that provide justification for rape—for example, the endorsement of beliefs that women unconsciously desire to be raped or beliefs that women who dress provocatively are asking to be raped (Lonsway and Fitzgerald, 1995). Many studies examining rape myth acceptance in men have administered a validated instrument referred to as the Rape Myth Acceptance Scale (RMAS; Burt, 1980). Studies using college student samples have found an association between high scores on either the RMAS or other measures of rape myth acceptance and sexual assault perpetration (DeGue, DiLillo, and Scalora, 2010; Locke and Mahalik, 2005; Zawacki et al., 2003).

A meta-analysis of studies examining the relationship between RMAS scores and a range of attitudes and behaviors found a strong relationship between RMAS scores and sexual aggression (Suarez and Gadalla, 2010). The study also found a significant correlation between RMAS scores and other measures of nonaggressive sexual behaviors, for example, sexually promiscuous behavior and the use of degrading images of women and a correlation with other prejudicial attitudes, such as racism, heterosexism, and ageism (Suarez and Gadalla, 2010). According to the authors, these findings suggest that sexual assault prevention programs should broaden their focus to address other forms of prejudice (e.g., racism) that were found to be correlated with high RMAS scores. To our knowledge, the effectiveness of this program strategy, however, has not yet been tested.

Some researchers have asserted that the RMAS overlaps the measurement of rape myth acceptance with hostility toward women, attitudes that would likely include rape myth acceptance (Lonsway and Fitzgerald, 1995). Other research has supported this assertion in finding that measures of rape myth acceptance and sexual aggression were negated when measures of hostility toward women were added as a covariate in the analysis. In other words, once hostility toward women (an attitude) was accounted for, rape myth acceptance (a cognition) was no longer predictive of sexual assault perpetration (Forbes et al., 2004). In response, a revised rape myth acceptance scale has been proposed, the Illinois Rape Myth Acceptance Scale (IRMA), in an attempt to address concerns with the RMAS (Payne, Lonsway, and Fitzgerald, 1999). The utility of the IRMA has not yet been fully vetted, and more research using the IRMA in sexual assault studies is needed (Adams-Curtis and Forbes, 2004).

Belief in Traditional Gender Roles

Studies have also examined a link between beliefs in traditional gender roles (that women and men should adhere to their respective traditional roles and traits) and sexual assault perpetration. Some studies have found a link between men in the general population who admit to having committed sexual assault and the endorsement of traditional gender roles (Carr and Van Deusen,

2004, and White et al., 2008). In another study, belief in traditional gender roles was the only significant predictor of sexual aggression when perceived token resistance (or reporting past sexual experiences in which the partner initially said he or she did not want to engage in sexual activity but eventually did) was included in the model (Loh et al., 2005). In this model, perceived token resistance and belief in traditional gender roles explained about 9 percent of the variance in whether someone engaged in sexually aggressive behavior or not (Loh et al., 2005).

Hypermasculinity

Other research has explored the relationship between hypermasculinity and sexual assault perpetration. Hypermasculine men have been conceptualized as possessing callous attitudes toward sex, experiencing excitement in the face of danger, and believing that expression of violence is manly (Mosher and Sirkin, 1984). These characteristics then predispose hypermasculine men to exert power and dominance over women, including exhibitions of sexual aggression. A number of studies have found an association between hypermasculinity and sexual assault perpetration (e.g., Gold et al., 1992; Mosher and Anderson, 1986; Parrott and Zeichner, 2003). Other research has found that hypermasculine men are more likely to display aggression toward women who violate traditional gender norms (Reidy et al., 2009), suggesting that hypermasculine men may be compelled to assert their dominance when they feel their masculinity has been threatened, in this case, through challenges to traditional gender roles.

Similar in concept is the construct referred to as *hostile masculinity* (developed by Malamuth et al., 1991). Hostile masculinity is defined as the need to control and dominate women, combined with hostility toward and distrust of women. It was found to be a significant pathway to sexual violence in a model of sexual aggression (Malamuth et al., 1995). A survey of community men found that those men who reported the highest levels of hostile masculinity were most likely to have perpetrated sexual violence (Greene and Davis, 2011). A meta-analysis of studies examining the relationship between various measures of masculine ideology and sexual aggression found both hypermasculinity and hostile masculinity to be moderately related to sexual aggression (Murnen, Wright, and Kaluzny, 2002).

Conclusion

Research has identified a number of different gender-related cognitions and attitudes that are associated with sexual assault perpetration. Some attitudes toward women, such as the belief in traditional gender roles and hostility toward women, have been linked to sexual assault perpetration. In addition, extreme attitudes and cognitions about masculinity have been found to be predictive of sexual assault perpetration. Finally, while several studies have found that the endorsement of rape myths is related to the commission of sexual assault, some researchers have argued that positive correlations in these studies are driven by measures of hostile and sexist attitudes toward women that are included in the research. While it could be argued that many of the gender-related cognitions examined thus far include some overlap, overall, the research does seem to indicate that attitudes and cognitions about gender play some role in sexual assault perpetration. More research is needed to tease apart the effects of each gender-related factor. In addition, studies should continue to explore the manner in which gender-related attitudes interact with other predictors, such as peer attitudes, alcohol, and sexual behavior.

Perceptions of Peer Attitudes and Behavior

Because sexual offenders have been hypothesized to be particularly influenced by the attitudes and behaviors of their peers (Abbey et al., 2006), a number of studies have explored the role of peer effects on sexual assault perpetration, specifically the effect of individuals' perceptions about their peers' attitudes toward and encouragement of sexual violence and their perceptions of whether their peers engage in sexual assault. Below, we summarize research looking at the influence of these peer-related factors on sexual assault perpetration.

A small number of studies have examined whether individuals who report having friends who engage in sexual aggression are more likely to then perpetrate sexual assault themselves. These studies have found an effect of peer sex aggression on sexual assault perpetration (Christopher, Madura, and Weaver, 1998, and DeKeseredy and Kelly, 1995). The actual level of sexual aggression by peers in these studies is not known; rather, these studies are measuring whether the level to which a person believes his or her friends are engaging in sexual aggression has an effect on the individual's decisions to engage in sexually aggressive behavior him- or herself.

Other studies have examined whether perceptions of peers' attitudes toward sexual assault are associated with the likelihood of having committed sexual assault. Several studies have found that individuals who perceive their peers as approving of sexual assault are more likely to commit sexual assault themselves (Abbey et al., 2007; Capaldi et al., 2001; Franklin, Bouffard, and Pratt, 2012; Humphrey and Kahn, 2000; Kingree and Thompson, 2013; Thompson et al., 2011). Other research, which used a sample of 652 male college students, found that men who reported perceiving norms among their peers that were supportive of sexual aggression were more likely to engage in sexually aggressive behavior one year later than men who did not report perceiving sexually aggressive norms (Thompson et al., 2011). One prospective study on adult perpetration found that adolescents who reported that their peers described women in derogatory terms were more likely than other men to engage in dating violence later as adults, including sexual violence (Capaldi et al., 2001). Other research has found that individuals who perceived peer pressure to engage in sexual activity in general were also more likely to perpetrate sexual assault (Abbey et al., 2007).

Finally, a recent longitudinal study examined the role of peer influences on sexual assault among male fraternity members. After gathering information on peer approval for sex, peer pressure for sex, alcohol use, and sexual behavior from a cohort of incoming freshmen over the course of three years, the study found that between the first and second year of college, men who joined a fraternity reported increases in reported perceptions of peer approval for forced sex and peer pressure to engage in sexual activity. In turn, increases in perceptions of peer approval for forced sex predicted sexual assault perpetration one year later (Kingree and Tompson, 2013). Other research with male fraternity members has found that fraternity members reported experiencing increased levels of pressure to engage in sexual activity, which in turn predicted the likelihood of sexual assault perpetration (Franklin, Bouffard, and Pratt, 2012).

Conclusion

Research on the effects of peer influences on sexual assault perpetration seems to indicate that an individual's perceptions of his peers' attitudes and behaviors about sex and sexual aggression are related to sexual assault perpetration. A number of studies have found that perceptions of peer approval of forced sex is related to sexual assault perpetration. A smaller number of studies have also identified a link between sexual assault perpetration and peer pressure to engage in sexual activity, as well as perceived peers' engagement in sexual aggression.

Substance Use

Alcohol consumption has been found to co-occur with sexual assault perpetration at a fairly high rate. Across studies, research estimates that in around 50 percent of sexual assaults, the victim, the perpetrator, or both individuals consumed alcohol prior to the assault (Abbey et al., 2001). In the past 20 years, a body of literature has emerged that has begun to explore the relationship between alcohol consumption (and to a lesser extent, drug use) and sexual assault. While some of the literature has focused on the experiences and outcomes of victims of alcohol/drug-related sexual assault (e.g., Kaysen et al., 2007; Lawyer et al., 2010; Mohler-Kuo et al., 2004), below we summarize the empirical literature more specifically examining the role of alcohol and drugs in the perpetration of sexual assault.

Alcohol Use

Research on the role of alcohol consumption in sexual assault perpetration has focused on two different mechanisms through which alcohol can have an effect: pharmacological and psychological (Abbey, 2011). Pharmacological mechanisms of alcohol consumption refer to a decrease in cognitive functioning due to alcohol consumption and to a decrease in inhibitions. After consuming alcohol, individuals lose sight of distal cues, such as empathy for the victim and the long-term consequences of their actions, and focus instead on more immediate cues, such as sexual arousal, anger, and frustration. This effect has been theorized to be more likely in men who are predisposed to sexual aggression (Abbey, 2002).

Psychological mechanisms of alcohol consumption refer to the interaction between perpetrators' beliefs about the effects of alcohol on their own behavior and the pharmacological effects of alcohol. In this respect, alcohol can affect how intoxicated individuals interpret behavior around them to conform to what they want to happen. For example, if an individual is looking to engage in sex, they may interpret a woman's willingness to dance as an invitation to have sex (Abbey, 2011).

Empirical research on the role of alcohol in sexual assault perpetration has generally employed one of two strategies: (1) experimental research conducted in a controlled laboratory setting in which participants are randomly assigned to drink alcohol or not and are asked to interpret sexual situation scenarios (Abbey, Zawacki, and Buck, 2005, and Marx, Gross, and Adams, 1999); or (2) surveys of a large group of individuals in which alcohol consumption and past sexual aggression are measured through self-reporting (Zawaki et al., 2003). Both methods of study have benefits and drawbacks. While a controlled experimental study allows researchers to draw causal conclusions about the effects of alcohol on sexual interpretations, the sterile laboratory environment makes it difficult to generalize to real-world settings, such as bars or parties. Surveys of a large group of participants can identify individuals who admit to previously committing sexual assault perpetration and measure their self-reported prior alcohol use, but this method identifies associations between alcohol and sexual assault only under particular circumstances and does not allow for causal statements about the effects of alcohol on sexual assault perpetration.

Studies specifically examining the effects of alcohol on sexual aggression within a laboratory setting have generally found that, compared with sober participants, participants who consumed alcohol were more likely to report beliefs conducive to sexual assault. For example, men's behaviors in presented scenarios were seen as appropriate, it was assumed that women enjoy forced sex, and women were seen to be willing to engage in those same forcible actions if they were in the presented situation (Marx, Gross, and Adams, 1999). Compared with sober participants, those who consumed alcohol were also found to be more likely to misperceive a woman's behavior as sexualized and inviting of sexual attention (Abbey et al., 2000 and 2005).

Other studies have employed survey methods to compare the characteristics of perpetrators of alcohol-related sexual assault and their behaviors to perpetrators who report committing sexual assault when sober. One survey compared the characteristics of three groups: individuals who did not admit to committing sexual assault, individuals who committed assault when either the victim or the perpetrator had consumed alcohol, and individuals who committed assault when neither the victim nor perpetrator had consumed alcohol. Alcohol-related and non-alcohol-related participants did not differ on any of the measured risk factors (e.g., delinquency, attitudes toward casual sex, hostility toward women) (Zawaki et al., 2003). Alcohol-related perpetrators were more likely to endorse beliefs that alcohol increased men's and women's sex drive and were more likely to report higher levels of overall alcohol consumption and higher levels of alcohol consumption during sexual situations.

Drug Use

Compared with research on alcohol, we know much less about the role of perpetrator drug use in sexual assault perpetration. One of the few studies to examine the relationship between drug use and sexual assault perpetration in the United States surveyed a sample of 851 college men five times over a four-year period about their frequency of drinking, marijuana use, other illicit drug use, and their participation in sexually aggressive behavior (Swartout and White, 2010). They found that, controlling for alcohol use, increases in drug use immediately before sexual activity over time predicted increases in the severity of sexual aggression.[5] More research is needed, however, to fully understand the relationship between perpetrator drug use and sexual assault perpetration.

Conclusion

The high rate at which alcohol consumption occurs in conjunction with sexual assault perpetration has led to a number of studies examining the link between alcohol and sexual assault perpetration. These studies seem to indicate that alcohol consumption can play a role in sexual assault perpetration. Some studies indicate that alcohol consumption increases men's misperceptions of women's sexual interest. Research on the association between drug use and sexual assault perpetration is sparse, and further research is needed to more fully understand the influence of various forms of drug use on sexual assault perpetration.

Integrated Models of Sexual Assault Perpetration

While many of the factors reviewed above have been found to be associated with sexual assault perpetration, on its own, no single perspective or factor is highly predictive of sexual assault perpetration. Recognizing the complexity of these offenses, researchers have more recently focused on developing models that consider a variety of possible factors that could influence sexual assault perpetration. Rather than relying on a single factor to try to explain sexual assault, recent efforts often rely on multiple theories about sexual assault perpetration and empirical data to guide theory development. Figure 2.1 shows one such model, the Confluence Model of Sexual Aggression (Malamuth et al., 1991 and 1995). The Confluence Model is one of the most frequently cited and tested theories of adult sexual assault perpetration within the recent literature. The Confluence Model considers developmental, attitudinal, and environmental factors and describes two pathways to sexual aggression—the *hostile-masculinity pathway* and the *impersonal-sex pathway*.

---

[5] A prior review (Tharp et al., 2013) identified an additional study that was conducted outside the United States, which found an association between sexual assault perpetration and some types of drugs but not others (Simbayi et al., 2006).

Figure 2.1. The Confluence Model of Sexual Aggression

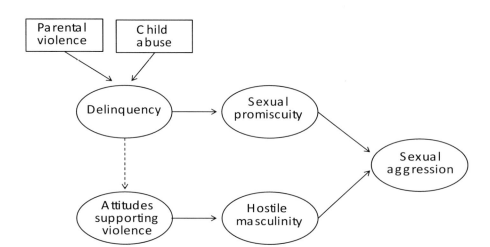

The *hostile-masculinity pathway* describes a series of events in which an individual who experiences violence during childhood through abuse and parental violence begins to associate with delinquent peers. Association with delinquent peers then leads to development of negative attitudes toward women and romantic relationships and to beliefs that women are sexual objects. The *impersonal-sex pathway* describes a process whereby abusive experiences in the home lead to associations with delinquent peers who encourage sexual promiscuity and conquests. This encouragement leads to early engagement in sexual activities, which increases opportunities to perpetrate sexual assault. The main difference between the two pathways is that one pathway works through negative attitudes and opinions about women, and the other through early and increased sexual experiences. While each of the pathways is proposed to independently predict sexual aggression, the Confluence Model also asserts that the pathways can interact to predict sexual aggression. According to the model, individuals who have both high hostile masculinity and high impersonal-sex scores should be most likely to display sexual aggression.

In the original test of the model, both pathways independently predicted acts of sexual aggression and explained 26 percent of the variance reports of the frequency and severity of sexual aggression. In addition, the interaction between hostile masculinity and impersonal sex explained an additional 4 percent of the variance in whether or not someone displayed sexual aggression.

Since its development, the Confluence Model has been tested several times with different populations and has been found to be predictive of sexual assault perpetration (Hall et al., 2005; and Malamuth et al., 1991 and 1995; and Malamuth, 1996). Researchers generally consider this to be a good model when trying to predict something as complex as human behavior because it explains about 30 percent of the variance in the frequency and severity of sexual aggression. To date, the Confluence Model is considered one of the best models developed; however, researchers are continuing to work to better explain its etiology.

Much of the continued integrated-theory development using empirical data within adult sexual assault perpetration has attempted to expand on the Confluence Model of sexual aggression. For example, other research has begun to examine the utility of including other factors in the model, such as empathy and alcohol consumption. These studies have found that inclusion of these factors also helps explain variation in sexual aggression, though the amount of sexual aggression explained by these expanded models stays generally around the levels found in the original model (Parkhill and Abbey, 2008, and Wheeler, George, and Dahl, 2002).

Research by Malamuth and others has suggested that there are some correlates and precursors to sexual aggression (which includes both legal and illegal behavior), but these studies were not designed to specifically predict who will or will not sexually assault at any particular time. Notably, the challenges of using different measures to predict future offending are well documented and have been studied for decades. For example, we know that many sex offenders were abused in the past, but that most abuse victims do not become sexual offenders. A key complication in using a test or series of tests to predict sexual assault proclivity is that, although the tests may be able to identify an increased risk for committing sexual assault, the overall risk of someone sexually assaulting another is low. Sexual assault perpetration, or sexual aggression that meets the legal definition of sexual assault/rape, has a lower base rate over any particular time period, and behaviors that have a low base rate are extremely difficult to predict. This may explain, in part, why Malamuth and others have focused on using the Confluence Model to predict sexually aggressive behaviors more broadly, rather than sexual assault more specifically.

The Characteristics of Sexual Assault Perpetrators in the Military

Most research on sexual assault perpetrator risk factors has been studied only in civilian adjudicated and/or community samples. While it seems likely that some or many of the risk factors observed within the civilian literature would also be related to likelihood of sexual-assault perpetration within the military, there is not a substantial body of research that has specifically studied, for example, whether hypermasculinity scores are significantly correlated with sexual assault perpetration in military samples.

One study with incoming Navy recruits surveyed individuals about their experiences with sexual assault (defined as attempted or complete rape) prior to joining the military (Stander et al., 2008). Thirteen percent of the more than 5,000 men surveyed reported having perpetrated sexual assault since reaching 14 years of age. The only significant factor associated with sexual assault perpetration was marital status; men who were married were least likely to report having perpetrated sexual assault (Stander et al., 2008). A longitudinal study of Navy recruits surveyed participants about their sexual assault experiences prior to entering the military as well as during their first year of military service (McWhorter et al., 2009). At one year of service, 13 percent of the sample reported perpetrating at least one incident of sexual assault since the age of 14; 9 percent reported only perpetrating sexual assault prior to joining the military, 2 percent reported perpetrating sexual assault both before and during military service, and another 2 percent reported only committing sexual assault while serving in the military. Of those who reported perpetrating sexual assault, 29 percent reported having committed a single assault, and 71 percent reported perpetrating two or more sexual assaults. No demographic characteristics or characteristics of the assault were found to be associated with the likelihood of sexual assault perpetration. The likelihood of perpetrating assault while in the military, however, was associated with sexual assault perpetration prior to joining the military. Men who reported having perpetrated assault prior to their military service were more than ten times more likely to perpetrate sexual assault in the military than men who did not report committing sexual assault prior to joining the military (McWhorter et al., 2009).

We do know some information about the characteristics of military sexual assault perpetrators and the circumstances surrounding these assaults through descriptive statistics gathered through the WGRA. Similar to the civilian literature, most sexual assault is perpetrated by men. According to the 2012 WGRA, of the 6.1 percent of active-duty women who reported experiencing unwanted sexual contact in 2012, 94 percent indicated that the perpetrator(s) was a man, and 5 percent reported that the assailants included both men and women (Rock, 2013). Similar to the civilian literature, alcohol is often consumed prior to assaults in the military; in 57 percent of incidents, either the offender or the victim consumed alcohol prior to the assault; the perpetrator or the victim used drugs in 2 percent of assaults (Rock, 2013). It should be noted that because women who reported having been victimized reported the characteristics of perpetrators, it is possible that the victims may not always have correctly remembered information about their perpetrators.

Predicting Sexual Assault Perpetration

Although research has identified a number of risk factors associated with sexual assault perpetration, our review of the literature did not find any tools that are currently in use to predict the likelihood of sexual assault perpetration within the general population. Individually, each risk factor is not highly predictive of sexual assault perpetration. Rather, as evidenced by the wide variety of factors that have been linked to sexual assault perpetration, it is likely a combination of factors that affect the likelihood of sexual assault perpetration. Furthermore, the combination of factors likely varies by individual.

Risk-assessment tools have been developed for use within the criminal-justice system to predict the likelihood of re-offense among convicted sexual assault perpetrators. Some of the most common risk-assessment tools for sex offenders include the Violence Risk Scale—Sex Offender Version (VRS-SO; Olver et al., 2007) and the Static-99 (Hanson and Thornton, 1999). These tools are used by criminal-justice professionals to make decisions, for example, about the necessity of civil commitment or the level of supervision required upon release. The latest generation of risk-assessment tools relies on both static (or historical) factors and dynamic-risk factors, or factors that could change in the offender's present situation, such as employment, social networks, and attitudes. Many of the factors assessed in these tools, however, would not be applicable to predicting offending in the general population or that of the Air Force, because they take into account offender-specific factors, such as victim characteristics, age at first offense, and responsiveness to treatment. Furthermore, meta-analyses of the accuracy of these tools indicate that the false-positive rate, or the rate at which the tools predict the person will re-offend when they do not, is around 30 percent, and the false-negative rate is even higher (Hanson and Morton-Bourgon, 2005, and Hanson and Bussière, 1998).

Other research in correctional settings has examined whether personality inventories, such as the Minnesota Multiphasic Personality Inventory-2 (MMPI-2; Butcher, 2001) or Personality Assessment Inventory (Morey, 1991) can distinguish between known sex offenders and non–sex offenders (Davis and Archer, 2010). Personality inventories are standardized, self-report tests that have traditionally been used in clinical settings to assess mental illness and sets of personality characteristics, but they have also been used by criminal-justice professionals to assess and treat known sex-offender populations (Grover, 2011). A review of existing empirical studies testing for differences in personality inventories between sex offenders and non-offenders found that the MMPI (i.e., an earlier version of the MMPI-2) was the most–commonly tested personality inventory with sex-offender populations (Davis and Archer, 2010). Looking across these studies, only one scale, the *Pd* scale, of the MMPI was consistently found to be elevated in known sex offenders compared with non–sex offenders. Because the *Pd* scale is associated with constructs related to antisocial behaviors such as lying, cheating, alcohol and drug use, and sexual acting out, researchers hypothesize that elevated *Pd* scales found in the sex-offender scales could simply more generally describe the criminal characteristics of these offenders as opposed to characteristics that are specific to sexual offending. In addition, these studies did not use the MMPI or other personality inventories to predict sex-assault perpetration within the general population; rather these studies were testing whether known, adjudicated sex offenders— a very specific sample within the universe of sexual assault perpetrators—are different from known non–sex offenders. Thus far, the research does not speak to the use of personality inventories to predict sexual assault perpetration within the general population.

Conclusion

A substantial amount of research has been devoted to understanding the characteristics of sexual assault perpetrators. To date, several different types of factors have been found to be associated with sexual assault perpetration. These include historical factors, such as abuse during childhood and prior sexual behavior; individual-level factors, such as gender-related attitudes and cognitions; and contextual factors, such as peer influences and alcohol and drug use. The wide range of factors identified thus far illustrates the complexity of sexual assault perpetration. To date, no single factor has been found to be highly predictive of sexual assault perpetration;

rather, combinations of these factors interact in a number of different ways to influence sexual assault perpetration.

Within the criminal-justice system, practitioners employ tools to predict risk of re-offense and to treat adjudicated sex offenders. These tools are not appropriate, however, for predicting the likelihood of sexual assault perpetration within the general population. While research has identified a number of risk factors for sexual assault within the general population, individually, each risk factor is not highly predictive of sexual assault perpetration. The complexity of factors influencing sexual assault perpetration and the multiple pathways that may lead an individual to commit a sexual assault would likely make it difficult to predict whether any one individual is likely to commit sexual assault in the future. In fact, even the most sophisticated and complex theories of offending can account for 30 percent of the variation in sexually aggressive behavior—ranging from no sexually aggressive behavior to frequent and serious sexual offending. These models do not, however, predict who will and will not be a sexual assault perpetrator. Therefore, the existing literature indicates there are likely significant challenges associated with the development of a screening tool that could reliably identify individuals within the general population who are at risk to perpetrate sexual assault.

3. Behaviors of Male Perpetrators Who Sexually Assault Female Victims

Some research on male perpetrators who sexually assault female victims has focused on understanding the behaviors of sexual assault perpetrators, including how they plan for the attack and common behavioral patterns they display during and after the attack. Much of what we know about behavioral patterns has been identified through studies comparing the behaviors of different forms of perpetration—for example, stranger versus acquaintance sexual assault. Below, we provide a summary of the literature examining the behavioral patterns of male perpetrators who sexually assault female victims.

Behaviors of Serial Perpetrators Who Sexually Assault Strangers

Some recent research on the behaviors of sexual assault perpetrators has focused on the decisionmaking process of serial sexual assault perpetrators who offend against strangers. Because stranger assaults are often the most difficult assaults for police to solve, these researchers have chosen to focus on the behaviors of serial-stranger sexual assault perpetrators in an effort to assist criminal-justice officials in profiling these types of offenders (Beauregard et al., 2007). While still a relatively new area of research, thus far studies have found that these perpetrators make a series of deliberate decisions about how, when, and where to hunt, target, and subdue their victims (Beauregard et al., 2007; Beauregard and Leclerc, 2007; Rebocho and Silva, 2014). Serial stranger-assault perpetrators make up a small percentage of the total population of sexual assault perpetrators, however, and likely possess different motivations, characteristics, and behaviors compared with individuals who perpetrate acquaintance assault. Therefore, this research is not likely to be generalizable to the behaviors and decisionmaking processes within the broader population of sexual assault perpetrators.

The Cycle of Sexual Offending

We were unable to identify a great deal of empirical research that has examined the decisionmaking processes of sexual assault perpetrators. One recently published book that reviews the empirical research on serial sexual assault perpetration provided a general description of the behavior of sexual assault perpetrators, referred to as the *cycle of sexual offending* (Terry, 2012). According to this description, the cycle of offending for sexual assault perpetrators includes planning on a conscious or unconscious level that occurs prior to the offense. Furthermore, the perpetrator's thoughts after the offense allow the individual to commit sexual assault again in the future (Terry, 2012). Below, we summarize this description in more detail.

Similar to the research on serial-stranger sexual assault perpetrators, prior to committing sexual assault, perpetrators make a series of decisions leading up to the offense. Often, however, they make what researchers refer to as a *series of seemingly irrelevant decisions* (SIDs) that eventually lead to the commission of a sexual assault (Terry, 2012). SIDs do not have to be sexual in nature. Rather, SIDs are decisions that, while not immediately relevant to perpetrating sexual assault, do eventually provide the offender with opportunities to come into contact with potential victims and commit sexual assault.

SIDs often intersect with other behaviors, feelings, and thoughts to act as triggers to the assault. Some triggers act as disinhibitors (i.e., factors that weaken inhibitions); for example, using alcohol or drugs or being in situations that provide access to vulnerable victims may provide the perpetrator with feelings that their actions are allowable or justified. Other triggers act as potentiators (i.e., factors that are conducive to particular actions), which, in the perpetrator's mind, "push" him toward aggressive sexual acts. Potentiators often include negative emotions, such as depression, loneliness, or humiliation. For example, a perpetrator feeling lonely and depressed may turn to alcohol to alleviate negative feelings. Once intoxicated, he may decide to go to a party in which he encounters a woman who is highly intoxicated and unable to fend off his sexual advances. The perpetrator may report that he was not consciously making the decision that night to go out and commit sexual assault. Regardless, the series of decisions he made led to the opportunity to perpetrate sexual assault, which he acted upon.

According to this description of the cycle of offending, following the assault, sexual assault perpetrators commonly display what are referred to as *cognitive distortions*, or thought processes that provide justification or excuses for their behavior (Murphy, 1990). These cognitive distortions, whether actually believed by the offender or not, allow the perpetrator to continue his behavior and potentially perpetrate sexual assault again. Many offenders engage in cognitive distortions by minimizing the seriousness of their actions, responsibility, and harm to the victim or by denying that the offense happened or that they planned to commit the act (Marshall et al., 1999).

Behaviors of Sexual Assault Perpetrators and Behavioral Differences Among Different Types of Perpetrators

To understand commonly employed tactics and behaviors of sexual assault perpetrators, several studies have asked college or community samples of men about the strategies they employed to carry out sexual acts, ranging from courtship behaviors to sexually aggressive behaviors that meet the legal criteria for rape (DeGue and DiLillo, 2005, and Senn et al., 2000). These studies typically find that those respondents who admit to sexually aggressive behavior typically use verbal threats or incapacitation, but less commonly admit to using physical force. One survey of

304 male college students found that 26.6 percent of their sample admitted to using verbal coercion to obtain sexual activity, and 5.9 percent indicated deliberately getting a woman too drunk to resist (DeGue and DiLillo, 2005). Additionally, 1.6 percent admitted to using physical force to kiss, fondle, or obtain oral sex, but none of the respondents reported using physical force to have sexual intercourse (DeGue and DiLillo, 2005). One survey with 195 community men found that 8.7 percent of the sample admitted to using verbal coercion to obtain sexual intercourse, 3.1 percent admitted to providing alcohol or drugs to incapacitate the victim, and 1 percent used physical force to obtain sex (Senn et al., 2000). In another survey of 115 community men, 16.5 percent of respondents reported using verbal coercion, 21.7 percent admitted to having sex with a woman who was too drunk to provide consent, and 7.8 percent reported using physical force or threats of physical force (Davis et al., 2008).

Other lines of research examining the behaviors of sexual assault perpetrators have compared tactics between particular types of sexual assault perpetrators—for example, between assaults against strangers versus acquaintance assaults. Some research has found that, prior to the assault, strangers are more likely to use blitz or surprise attacks or to kidnap the victim (Woods and Porter, 2008), whereas acquaintance rapists are more likely to use opportunistic approaches, such as when the victim is sleeping, intoxicated, or drugged (Stermac, Du Mont, and Kalemba, 1995), or to use trust approaches to gain the victim's compliance (Woods and Porter, 2008). Perpetrators of stranger assaults are more likely to commit the assault outdoors compared with acquaintance rapists, who are more likely to commit the assault indoors, most commonly in the perpetrator's or the victim's home (Jones et al., 2004; Stermac, Du Mont, and Kalemba, 1995). One study of victims' reports of rapists found that acquaintance rape perpetrators were more likely to act alone compared with stranger rapists (Koss et al., 1988). The study found no difference in victims' perceived use of alcohol or drugs on the part of the perpetrator; most perpetrators were reportedly using alcohol, drugs, or both at the time of the assault, regardless of assault type (Koss et al., 1988). More research is needed, however, to know whether this study's findings are replicable among other samples of acquaintance and stranger sexual assault perpetrators.

Research seems to indicate that, during the assault, perpetrators of stranger assaults display more hostile behaviors, including verbal aggression, threats of bodily harm, and physical violence, and are more likely to use a weapon during the attack compared with acquaintance assault perpetrators (Bownes, O'Gorman, and Sayers, 1991; Koss et al., 1988; Stermac, Du Mont, and Kalemba, 1995; Woods and Porter, 2008). Some research also indicates that victims of stranger attacks sustain more non-genital injuries (Jones et al., 2004).

Other research compared the tactics of sober and light-consumption perpetrators (i.e., one to four drinks prior to the incident) to those of heavy drinkers (i.e., five or more drinks during the incident; Parkhill, Abbey, and Jacques-Tiura, 2009). This research found that, controlling for perpetrators' typical level of drinking and the victims' level of intoxication, compared with sober or light drinkers, heavy drinkers were more likely to use behavioral tactics to control and isolate their victims and to use more physical force during the assaults (Parkhill, Abbey, and Jacques-Tiura, 2009).

Other research has examined the behavioral and situational factors surrounding alcohol-related assault compared with sober assaults. This line of research has found alcohol-consuming perpetrators to be more likely to assault a casual acquaintance and to report that the assault was unplanned after having spent time together at a social event (Abbey et al., 2003, and Ullman, 1999a). Some research has found that alcohol consumption is related to more physically aggressive or violent assaults compared with sober assaults, but findings are mixed, possibly because studies failed to measure the amount of alcohol consumed prior to the attack (Brecklin and Ullman, 2001; Ullman and Brecklin, 2000; Abbey, 2011). Some research has further examined whether the amount of alcohol consumed during perpetration is related to the level of perpetrator aggression during the assault (Abbey et al., 2003). This study found that, as the number of drinks increased from zero to four, the level of aggression during sexual assault increased. The level of aggression then stayed steady until nine drinks, then at nine or more drinks, the level of aggression declined—presumably because, at this level of intoxication, cognitive and motor functioning would be significantly impaired.

Behaviors of Sexual Assault Perpetrators in the Military

According to the 2012 WGRA, similar to civilian sexual assault, most military victims are assaulted by someone they know (Rock, 2013). Overall, 90 percent of female service members reported they were assaulted by someone they knew. Fifty-seven percent of assailants were reported to be military coworkers, and 40 percent were reported as other military personnel. Smaller percentages of assailants were individuals within the local community (8 percent), a spouse or significant other (7 percent), or a Department of Defense/service-civilian employee or contractor (9 percent). Unique to the military, respondents also reported the perpetrator's rank. Thirty-eight percent of assailants were higher ranking and not in the victim's chain of command, 25 percent were higher ranking and in the victim's chain of command, and 13 percent were subordinates. Sixty-seven percent of assaults against female victims occurred at a military installation, and 41 percent of the assaults happened during the work day/duty hours.

The 2012 WGRA also provides some information about perpetrators' behaviors during the assaults. Different than reports in the civilian literature that found small proportions of assaults using physical force, 50 percent of perpetrators who assaulted female victims used some degree of physical force, 17 percent threatened to ruin the victim's reputation, and 12 percent threatened to physically harm the victim (Rock, 2013). Three percent of female victims reported that the perpetrator used drugs to knock them out. Finally, 30 percent of female victims reported that the perpetrator sexually harassed them before or after the assault, 8 percent reported that the perpetrator stalked them before or after the assault; 20 percent reported that the perpetrator both sexually harassed and stalked them (Rock, 2013).

In a survey of Navy recruits who reported having committed sexual assault (i.e., rape or attempted rape) prior to their military service, between 18 and 21 percent of perpetrators reported exclusively using force or the threat of force, between 39 percent and 46 percent reported relying only on alcohol or drugs to perpetrate the assault, and between 32 and 43 percent reported using both force and alcohol or drugs during their assaults (Stander et al., 2008). Another study of sexual assault perpetration and re-perpetration among Navy service members, both before joining the military and during their first year of service, found that 75 percent of perpetrators committed sexual assault against only victims they knew. Seven percent reported perpetrating assault against only strangers, and another 18 percent reported having committed assault against both strangers and known victims (McWhorter et al., 2009). When looking at methods of attack and type of victim, researchers found that most perpetrators did not report using force to perpetrate sexual assault against a stranger. All men who reported using force against their victims targeted known victims. Men who targeted strangers reported using alcohol or drugs to perpetrate the assault.

Conclusion

While some research has focused on understanding the decisionmaking process and behavioral patterns of serial perpetrators who assault stranger victims, there is less empirical research examining the decisionmaking process of other types of perpetrators—for example, individuals who perpetrate assault against acquaintances. One general description of perpetration describes a cycle of offending, in which perpetrators plan the offense, perpetrate the act, and engage in a thought process following the act to justify or minimize their actions. While not all perpetrators consciously plan the attack, this description suggests that they engage in a series of decisions that lead to opportunities to commit sexual assault. Research has also identified some behavioral differences during the attack based on the type of perpetrators or the circumstances surrounding the attack. Descriptive statistics from the WGRA indicate that while some behaviors within the general population are similar to the behaviors of perpetrators in the military, victims report the use of physical force during the attack more frequently than offenses with civilians. An understanding of behaviors of sexual assault perpetrators—for example, the situations, feelings, and cognitions commonly leading up to the attack—are important to consider when devising prevention efforts.

4. Female Sexual Assault Perpetrators

There has been increasing interest in recent years to understand female sex offenders. Research on female sex offenders is a fairly new area of study and, as a consequence, most existing research is exploratory in nature and often not methodologically sophisticated. Most studies examine very small sample sizes, which limits the generalizability of findings. For example, a 2006 review of the literature on female sex offenders was able to identify only 13 empirical studies conducted between 1989 to 2004 that included sample sizes over ten (Johansson-Love and Fremouw, 2006). Furthermore, of the 13 studies identified, only eight compared female sex offenders to a control group. Without a comparison group, we cannot draw conclusions about whether any factors found in female sex offender populations occur with any more or less frequency than male sex offenders. In addition, most samples have been drawn from incarcerated populations or from clinical settings. These settings likely represent a very specific subset of offenders and do not provide information on the full range of possible female offenders. Finally, similar to the male-offender literature, these studies differed in their definitions and measurement of variables, including definitions of sexual assault.

Due to the paucity of studies and to the methodological issues present in existing studies, there is not yet consensus in the field on common characteristics and behaviors of female offenders. In addition, the majority of research has focused on female perpetrators who assault children or juveniles. Therefore, the literature described below should be interpreted with caution.

Frequency of Sexual Assault by Female Sexual Assault Perpetrators

It is difficult to know the exact incidence rate of sexual assault against adults perpetrated by women. Currently, national statistics of female sexual assault perpetration include perpetrations against minors and adults. Criminal-justice data indicate that less than 10 percent of sex crimes reported to authorities are perpetrated by women, and only 6 percent of all adult arrestees for sex crimes are women (Federal Bureau of Investigation, 2006). These figures may not accurately represent the proportion of female sexual assault perpetrators, however, as research indicates that sex crimes, including crimes committed by female offenders, are often not reported to authorities. Data collected by the National Crime Victimization Survey suggest that approximately 6 percent of all single-perpetrator sexual assaults are committed by a woman (Rand and Catalano, 2006).[6] In addition, in approximately 10 percent of rapes committed by

---

[6] Data from National Intimate Partner and Sexual Violence Survey suggest that 22 percent of men experience sexual violence victimization during their lives, but most male victims (93 percent) report perpetration by only men (Black et al., 2011).

more than one perpetrator, at least one offender is a woman (Rand and Catalano, 2006). We know little about incidence rates of female sexual assault perpetration in the military. According to the 2012 WGRA, 1 percent of female victims of unwanted sexual contact reported that the perpetrator(s) were only female, and 5 percent reported that the perpetrators were both male and female. For male victims, the gender of the perpetrator was not reportable.

Typologies of Female Sexual Assault Perpetrators

Existing research on the characteristics of female offenders seems to indicate that, like male sexual assault perpetrators, women who commit sexual assault are a heterogeneous group (Vandiver and Kercher, 2004). Therefore, much of the early research has focused on developing typologies of female sexual assault perpetrators (e.g., Mathews, Matthews, and Speltz, 1989). Most early typologies, however, were generated from observations of a small sample of offenders and did not include women who offend against other adults (Vandiver and Kercher, 2004).

One of the more recent typologies relied on a larger sample of 471 registered female sex offenders in Texas (Vandiver and Kercher, 2004). Using demographic information about the offenders and victims, the researchers used a statistical technique referred to as *cluster analysis* to identify six distinct subtypes. Only one of these six subtypes, *aggressive homosexual offenders*, included women who assaulted other adults. These perpetrators ($n = 17$) were on average 31 years of age, and the majority of their victims were women.

While very few of the offenders identified in these typologies include women who perpetrate sexual assault against adults, because of the populations used, it would be difficult to say that these typologies are representative of the entire population of female sexual assault perpetrators. It is possible that female perpetrators found in prisons or in clinical populations are a specific type of offender—for example, women who offend against children.

Characteristics of Female Sexual Assault Perpetrators

Because the study of female sexual assault perpetration is relatively new, thus far only a small number of possible characteristics have been examined with any frequency. It should be noted that all of the research we reviewed for this chapter includes at least some female perpetrators who assaulted children in their samples. Therefore, readers should employ caution when generalizing findings to female perpetrators who assault adults.

Prior Sexual Victimization

One of the most common factors studied as a predictor of female sex offending is prior sexual victimization experienced by the female sexual offender. Studies examining the characteristics of female offenders found that a large percentage, more than 75 percent, of female sex offenders report having previously been sexually abused (Lewis and Stanley, 2000, and Nathan and Ward, 2002). These studies relied on small sample sizes, however, so these percentages should be interpreted with caution.

Some research indicates that, compared with other types of offenders, women convicted of sex offenses have been previously victimized at higher rates. For example, one study using a clinical population found higher rates of self-reported prior childhood victimization in female sex offenders compared with both male sex offenders and non–sex offender women (Johansson-Love and Fremouw, 2006). These results should be interpreted with caution, as 18 female sex offenders were compared with 332 male sex-offenders and 125 female non–sex offenders. Two pre-2000 studies have found that female sexual assault perpetrators report higher rates of prior victimization compared with female college students (Fromuth and Conn, 1997). This study, however, largely focused on women who assaulted victims age 18 and younger.

Psychiatric History

Several studies have examined the relationship between mental illness and female sexual assault perpetration. Some exploratory studies report that female sexual assault perpetrators display high rates of mental illnesses, including depression, anxiety, posttraumatic stress disorder, substance abuse, and psychosis (Lewis and Stanley, 2000, and Nathan and Ward, 2002). Some of these studies, however, draw from clinical populations or from populations of offenders who were referred for competency-to-stand-trial evaluations, which may increase the likelihood of finding psychiatric illnesses. In addition, these studies have produced mixed findings, with some studies identifying an increased likelihood of a particular type of mental illness and others failing to find an association. More research is needed to fully understand the relationship between mental illness and female sexual assault perpetration.

Behaviors of Female Sexual Assault Perpetrators

To date, we know very little about the behaviors of female sexual assault perpetrators who assault other adults. One study examining a sample of 279 incarcerated female offenders who had sexually assaulted either an adult or a child/adolescent found that approximately 86 percent employed some degree of physical force to carry out the assault (Ferguson and Meehan, 2005). The generalizability of these results is questionable, however, as it is possible that offenders who display force and/or cause injury to the victim are more likely to be incarcerated for their offense.

Other research has examined college women's coercive approaches to obtain sexual activity from men (Anderson et al., 2005; Anderson and Newton, 2004; Struckman-Johnson, Struckman-Johnson, and Anderson, 2003). For example, one study surveyed 656 college men and women about their experiences as both perpetrators and victims of sexual-coercion tactics after an initial refusal for sex (Struckman-Johnson, Struckman-Johnson, and Anderson, 2003). Twenty-seven percent of the women surveyed indicated they had previously employed at least one sexually coercive tactic. Most of the women perpetrators reported using some form of nonphysical tactic, and within this sample, 25 percent engaged in behaviors designed to induce physical arousal (e.g., removing their own or the victims' clothing), 15 percent reported using some form of emotional manipulation (e.g., threats to break up, telling lies), about 5 percent reported either taking advantage of an intoxicated victim or getting the victim drunk, and 2.6 percent reported using some sort of physical force or threat of physical force (Struckman-Johnson, Struckman-Johnson, and Anderson, 2003). Another study surveyed college women residing in both urban and rural Southern and Midwestern regions of the United States about physical, nonphysical, and persuasion strategies they used to obtain sex (Anderson el al., 2005). They did not find differences in women's reported strategies based on their geographic location. There were a few differences in women's strategies based on their sexual and relationship histories. Women who used persuasion strategies (e.g., giving the man a massage) had had fewer sexual partners than women who reported using nonphysical (e.g., threats) or physical (e.g., hitting) strategies. Women who used nonphysical strategies reported a younger age at which they first had intercourse compared with women who used persuasion strategies. Women who reported using physical force to obtain sex had intercourse for the first time at a younger age than women who used persuasion or nonphysical strategies. Women who reported using physical force also reported calling a higher number of boys more frequently during their teenage years compared with the other two groups (Anderson et al., 2005).

One of the most consistent behavioral findings in the literature is the high rate at which adjudicated female sexual assault perpetrators co-offend, usually with one or more male partners (Rand and Catalano, 2006). One study of 277 women arrested for a sexual offense found that almost 50 percent committed the offense with another person (Vandiver, 2006). Other studies have identified high rates of co-offending female sexual assault perpetrators (Nathan and Ward, 2002). The majority of cases discussed, however, involve assaults conducted by adjudicated offenders against adolescents or children. It is unclear how many co-offending assaults are committed against other adults or in non-adjudicated samples.

Conclusion

The study of female sexual assault perpetrators is still emerging, with many fewer studies than the research on male-female sexual assault. In addition, most existing research has focused on the characteristics and behaviors of female offenders who commit assaults against children or adolescents. This focus on women who assault minors may be because many of the existing studies rely on clinical or incarcerated samples. Because of the stigma men may experience by being assaulted by a woman, these samples may not accurately capture the full range of situations in which women perpetrate sexual assault. Due to these limitations, there is currently little consensus on the characteristics or behaviors of female sexual assault perpetrators, especially those that offend against other adults.

5. Male Perpetrators Who Sexually Assault Male Victims

Historically, there has been little recognition of sexual assault perpetrated by men against other men. Societal beliefs—for example, myths that men could not be raped and men who were raped must be gay—perpetuated the lack of recognition of this issue. As a result, our empirical knowledge of sexual assault perpetrated by men against other adult men is sparse. In recent years, some studies have begun to explore the issue of sexual assault perpetrations by men against other men. The research on this type of sexual assault, however, is still mostly exploratory in nature, and we still do not have a complete picture of its prevalence, the characteristics of these types of perpetrators, or the circumstances surrounding these assaults.

In addition, much of the early research on male perpetrators who sexually assault other men simply described the incidents, rather than comparing the perpetration to a control group. Without a control group, we cannot know whether the characteristics observed in the study sample are more or less likely to occur compared with individuals who do not commit male-male sexual assault. Other studies included small sample sizes and/or relied on convenience samples that most likely do not represent the full range of this type of sexual assault. If a sample is gathered by convenience (e.g., a group of men that arrive at a sexual assault support group) or is very small, we cannot know if these results are generalizable to the rest of the population of male perpetrators who assault other men. Below, we describe the handful of recent studies that have begun to shed light on male perpetrators who sexually assault male victims. Due to the limitations of existing research, however, results should be interpreted with caution.

Frequency of Sexual Assault by Male Perpetrators Against Male Victims

It is difficult to know the exact prevalence rates of sexual assault by male perpetrators against male victims. While some studies of male sexual assault specify the gender of the perpetrator, many do not (Peterson et al., 2011). One nationally representative survey estimated that 1.7 percent of men in the United States have been sexually assaulted during their lifetime (Breiding et al., 2014). Of the reported cases of male rape, 79.3 percent of victims reported only male perpetrators (Breiding et al., 2014).

Typologies of Male Perpetrators Who Sexually Assault Male Victims

The existing research on the characteristics and behaviors of male perpetrators seems to indicate that they are a heterogeneous group, meaning there does not appear to be one single profile of a male perpetrator who sexually assaults male victims. Research examining known cases of male-on-male sexual assault has generally identified two different types of perpetrators based on their motivations for committing the assault (e.g., Almond, McManus, and Ward, 2013; Hickson et al., 1994; Hodge and Canter, 1998). The first group consists of homosexual men who commit assault against other homosexual men primarily for intimacy or sexual gratification. The second group consists of heterosexual men who commit sexual assault against other men as an expression of social dominance or control. Presumably, social-dominance assaults could be committed against homosexual men as an expression of bias or disapproval of their sexual orientation or against another man as a form of social dominance within a particular group, regardless of the victim's sexual orientation.

In one classification analysis of a sample of male-on-male sexual assault cases, those incidents classified as heterosexual men committing assault for dominance/control were more likely to be stranger attacks and include multiple perpetrators (Hodge and Canter, 1998). Perpetrators who committed assaults for sexual gratification or intimacy were more likely to have had prior social interactions or interpersonal relationships with their victim (Hodge and Canter, 1998). While more research is needed to gain a better understanding of the full range of male perpetrators who sexually assault male victims, these studies indicate that, similar to other types of sexual assault perpetrators, the motivations, characteristics, and behaviors of these perpetrators are complex and likely vary between perpetrators.

Characteristics of Male Perpetrators Who Sexually Assault Male Victims

Because the study of male-on-male sexual assault is still an emerging area of research, we know very little about the characteristics of male perpetrators who sexually assault other men. Most studies have simply provided descriptive accounts of the events. These studies have often drawn on relatively small samples of individuals from specific populations, such as emergency rooms or psychiatric facilities. Therefore, the generalizability of these descriptive accounts is limited. In addition, most studies have not examined the association between perpetrators and the types of characteristics often found to be related to other types of sexual assault.

Ongoing research has examined sexual assault victimization among active-duty members of the armed forces (Morral et al., 2015). Approximately 70 percent of victimized men responding to questions regarding the most serious offense they had experienced in the past year indicated that their offenders were men or a mixture of men and women. In addition, 34 percent of victimized men indicated that the incident was a form of hazing. Additional research is needed to more thoroughly consider the extent to which hazing may provide a context for male-on-male sexual violence.[7] More research is also needed on the characteristics of various types of male perpetrators who sexually assault other men.

---

[7] One of the only studies examining the characteristics associated with male perpetrators who assault other men included a survey conducted of 310 homosexual men residing in Germany. It found that homosexual men who reported engaging in sexually aggressive acts were more likely to report experiencing abuse as a child (physical, sexual, or emotional), to have previously accepted money for sex or paying money for sex, to have their first homosexual experience at a younger age, and to report that they would rape a man if they would not be caught or

Behaviors of Male Perpetrators Who Sexually Assault Male Victims

Studies on the behavior of male perpetrators who assault other men have drawn samples from different populations—for example, sexual assaults reported to police, emergency-room visits, or other clinical samples. In addition, some studies have focused exclusively on sexual assaults in which the victims and/or perpetrators are homosexual, and others have not differentiated their sample by sexual orientation. As a result, findings between studies are often mixed.

For example, some research found that most perpetrators know their victims and rarely use weapons during the attack, while other studies, using samples of victims who visited emergency rooms, reported high numbers of male-on-male sexual assaults perpetrated by a stranger who employed a weapon during the attack (Frazier, 1993, and Isely and Gehrenbeck-Shim, 1997). Studies have also varied in the reported proportion of assaults in which the perpetrator uses enough force to cause injury to the victim, ranging from 25 to 60 percent of assaults (Frazier, 1993, and Stermac et al., 1996). One study examining sexual assaults perpetrated by both homosexual and heterosexual perpetrators, which used surveys of victims and official police reports (Hodge and Cantor, 1998), found quite a bit of variation in the behaviors of the perpetrator and circumstances surrounding the attack: 64 percent of the assaults were perpetrated by more than one offender; 43 percent of the assaults were perpetrated within the victim's house or car, with the majority of the remaining assaults occurring outdoors; and 45 percent of homosexual victims and 36 percent of heterosexual victims were seriously injured during the course of the attack. In addition, assaults committed by a stranger were more likely to be reported by the police. These findings point to the need for research that considers both the source of data and male-on-male perpetration type.

Conclusions

The study of male perpetrators who sexually assault other men is still emerging. Existing studies do indicate that the motivations behind this type of sexual assault can vary. More research that considers differences among various types of male perpetrators who sexually assault other men is needed. In addition, most existing studies are largely descriptive in nature and/or are limited to particular samples. Therefore, more rigorous research examining the characteristics and behaviors among this diverse group of offenders is also needed.

---

punished, compared with homosexual men who did not report sexual aggression (Krahé, Scheinberger-Olwig, and Schütze, 2001).

6. Multiple-Perpetrator Sexual Assault

Multiple-perpetrator sexual assault involves a sexual assault in which more than one individual conducts the offense (Horvath and Kelly, 2009). The frequency of multiple-perpetrator sexual assault remains unclear, in part due to numerous issues in reporting and recording of sexual assault in general (Koss, 1993). Estimates for the United States suggest that the proportion of sexual assaults that involve multiple perpetrators ranges from 2 to 33 percent (da Silva, Woodhams, and Harkins, 2013, and Horvath and Kelly, 2009). According to the 2012 WGRA, 26 percent of women service members who reported unwanted sexual contact in 2012 were assaulted by multiple offenders (Rock, 2013). The percentage of male service-member victims who were assaulted by multiple offenders was not reportable because fewer than 15 respondents reported this experience or because the relative standard error was high.

Research on multiple-perpetrator sexual assault is limited and typically involves analysis of a select number of case descriptions, which are obtained through law enforcement or news reports (Porter and Alison, 2006). These reports are only available for reported cases, so the generalizability of information from these reports to unreported incidents is unclear. In addition, inconsistencies can be seen across studies, depending on the cases selected for inclusion in particular studies (Harkins and Dixon, 2010). Further, data from these reports often focus on victim statements (Chambers, Horvath, and Kelly, 2010), so there is little information on the interpersonal or intergroup dynamics of the offenders. With these limitations in mind, this chapter focuses on reviewing the past research and literature on multiple-perpetrator sexual assault, which may assist with preventing multiple-perpetrator sexual assault among those in the Air Force.

Descriptive Characteristics of Multiple-Perpetrator Sexual Assault

Descriptive research on multiple-perpetrator sexual assault suggests that most involve between two and four male offenders and that the victims tend to be women (Chambers, Horvath, and Kelly, 2010; Harkins and Dixon, 2010; Woodhams and Cooke, 2013). Incidents involving up to 22 offenders during a single multiple-perpetrator sexual assault have been recorded (Morgan, Brittain, and Welch, 2012). Although research on the characteristics of multiple-perpetrator sexual assaults is mixed (Harkins and Dixon, 2010), studies tend to show that multiple-perpetrator sexual assaults commonly begin with an offender approaching the victim at an outdoor location, then using a vehicle to move the victim to a private dwelling, with some research showing this occurring in more than 40 percent of reviewed assaults (Horvath and Kelly, 2009; Morgan, Brittain, and Welch, 2012; Porter and Alison, 2006; Ullman, 1999b). When approaching the victim, perpetrators tend to talk with and trick the victim into temporarily trusting them (da Silva et al., 2013). Thus, the initial encounter between one of the offenders and the victim is often friendly, then the victim is lured to a location, where the other offenders are located (Chambers, Horvath, and Kelly, 2010, and Morgan, Brittain, and Welch, 2012). The sexual assault then occurs at this new location. Of note, surprise attacks also occur with frequency in multiple-perpetrator sexual assaults (e.g., surprise used in 60 percent of these assaults; Porter and Alison, 2006).

Although some research suggests that there may be differences between multiple-perpetrator sexual assaults involving two offenders and those involving three or more offenders (da Silva, Woodhams, and Harkins, 2013), theory and research generally suggest that a leader, or one offender, tends to direct the actions of the other or group of others during multiple-perpetrator sexual assaults (Porter, 2013; Porter and Alison, 2001; Woodhams et al., 2012). During the offense, use of violence appears to be somewhat more common in multiple-perpetrator sexual assaults than in lone-perpetrator sexual assaults (Morgan, Brittain, and Welch, 2012, and Porter and Alison, 2006). The results of research on use of weapons during multiple-perpetrator sexual assaults are mixed, however, such that some studies have shown greater use of weapons in multiple-perpetrator sexual assaults than in lone-perpetrator sexual assaults (Hauffe and Porter, 2009, and Porter and Alison, 2006) and others have not (Morgan, Brittain, and Welch, 2012). Completed vaginal rape is common in all multiple-perpetrator sexual assaults, and it is more common in multiple-perpetrator sexual assaults than in lone-perpetrator sexual assaults (Morgan, Brittain, and Welch, 2012, and Ullman, 1999b).

Limited research suggests that, following the multiple-perpetrator sexual assault, approximately half of the victims may be released by the offenders, but approximately one-fifth of the victims are killed (Porter and Alison, 2006). The outcomes in the remainder of cases include victim escape (11 percent), victim rescue (8 percent), or unsuccessful attempts to kill the victim (3 percent). Of those released, approximately one-fourth are abandoned at the scene of the crime, and approximately one-fifth are transported elsewhere and then abandoned (Porter and Alison, 2006).

Characteristics of Multiple-Perpetrator Sexual Assault Offenders

Multiple-perpetrator sexual assault offenders tend to be either strangers or casual acquaintances of the victim (Morgan, Brittain, and Welch, 2012), so the victim is unlikely to have a close relationship with any of the multiple-perpetrator sexual assault offenders. On average, multiple-perpetrator sexual assault offenders are younger than lone offenders. Their average age tends to be approximately 21 to 22 years (Hauffe and Porter, 2009, and Ullman, 1999b), and they tend to choose victims who are approximately their same age or slightly younger (Porter and Alison, 2006). In addition, multiple-perpetrator sexual assault offenders are significantly more likely than lone-perpetrator sexual assault offenders to have a history of drug or alcohol abuse (Hauffe and Porter, 2009).

Social Contexts in Multiple-Perpetrator Sexual Assault

Keeping in mind that most multiple-perpetrator sexual assaults involve male offenders and female victims, multiple-perpetrator sexual assault may be more likely to occur in environments that encourage male bonding and group initiation through anti-female rituals, objectification of women, sexual violence, and norms of secrecy and cohesion (Harkins and Dixon, 2010). A culture or subculture that encourages sexual inequalities and violence may influence sexual perceptions and behaviors. Fraternities, gangs, and military groups have been analyzed in the context of promoting a culture of hypermasculinity, male dominance, and male bonding (Bourgois, 1996; Franklin, 2013; Harkins and Dixon, 2010; Lilly, 2007). This culture, coupled with other group components, including group loyalty and protection, may contribute to a greater likelihood of multiple-perpetrator sexual assault (Martin and Hummer, 1989).

Sexual assault of group members against other same-sex members in a group that encourages bonding and loyalty, such as during hazing activities, is also possible, but the frequency of this and factors that contribute to this are under-researched (Kirby and Wintrup, 2002). For example, multiple-perpetrator sexual assault or rape against a group initiate may occur in an effort to force the initiate to demonstrate their obedience and commitment to the group (Anderson, McCormack, and Lee, 2012). Due to the unwillingness of perpetrators and victims to report these acts, however, little research is available on this topic.

Social Psychological Processes in Multiple-Perpetrator Sexual Assault

Due to the involvement of more than one offender, perpetration in multiple-perpetrator sexual assault may be considered in the context of research on social processes. Interpersonal and group involvement appears to result, in part, from individual needs to belong and form bonds with others (Baumeister and Leary, 1995). In an effort to belong, a person may evaluate their own beliefs and actions against the beliefs and actions of others, including those of the group they wish to gain or maintain membership in (Festinger, 1954). If there is correspondence between the individual and group beliefs or behaviors, beliefs or behaviors may become more extreme (Myers, 1978). This would suggest that correspondence between mildly sexually violent thoughts and actions among those in a group may contribute to the performance of more extreme behaviors, including multiple-perpetrator sexual assault. Other theories support a related notion of group polarization through conformity to group norms (e.g., Mackie, 1986). If there is no correspondence between the individual and the group, the group may pressure or threaten the individual to conform, and thus, an individual may be pressured into engaging in multiple-perpetrator sexual assault (Harkins and Dixon, 2010).

Another social-psychological process often attributed to offender participation in multiple-perpetrator sexual assault is that of deindividuation (Harkins and Dixon, 2010). De-individuation involves a loss of individuality and a loss of self-awareness or self-monitoring. This may be more likely to arise when individuals perceive little personal responsibility (e.g., diffusion of responsibility), a great deal of anonymity, and when they have consumed drugs or alcohol (Fiske, 2004). Offenders may participate in multiple-perpetrator sexual assault because they perceive themselves as being subsumed by the group and lose their sense of self.

Multiple-Perpetrator Sexual Assault in the Military

A handful of other studies have explored the characteristics of multiple-perpetrator sexual assault in the military. In one international sample involving 223 offenses collected from archival sources dating from 1945 to 2001, 22 percent of offenses involved offenders who were currently in or had been in the military (Porter and Alison, 2006). Most of the military members involved in multiple-perpetrator sexual assault conducted the offenses on U.S. Army bases against U.S. Army women. Notably, most offenders with a military background were involved in cases dating from 1945 to 1979, with fewer involved in multiple-perpetrator sexual assault from 1980 to 2001. This suggests temporal changes in the involvement of military members in multiple-perpetrator sexual assault following the shift to an all-volunteer force.

Other research examining previous multiple-perpetrator sexual assault among military members during World War II found that these individuals were noncareer soldiers (e.g., drafted or volunteered during wartime) who tended to have mental-health concerns and low intelligence (Lilly, 2007). Further, it was suggested that a combination of combat stress and poor oversight of these individuals contributed to the assaults.

Conclusion

Although research on multiple-perpetrator sexual assault is limited, extant studies suggest that many of the characteristics of multiple-perpetrator sexual assault and multiple-perpetrator sexual assault offenders differ from those of lone-perpetrator sexual assault. As such, it is worthwhile to consider multiple-perpetrator sexual assault as separate and distinct from lone-perpetrator sexual assault. Research suggests that young men in hypermasculine, limited-oversight contexts who are under the influence of substances may be more likely to engage in multiple-perpetrator sexual assault. Various group processes, including polarization and de-individuation, may contribute to acceptance and performance of multiple-perpetrator sexual assault.

7. Conclusions and Implications for Prevention Efforts

To assist the Air Force in its continued efforts to combat sexual assault, we conducted a review of recent empirical literature on adult perpetrators who sexually assault other adults. The primary objective of this report was to synthesize what is empirically known about sexual assault perpetrator risk factors and behaviors for the Air Force. Our second aim was to highlight important findings within the literature that could inform ongoing and future sexual assault prevention and training efforts within the Air Force. Finally, we examined this literature to discern whether any tools existed that the Air Force could use in the recruitment screening of airmen to weed out sexual assault perpetrators. Below, we discuss several overarching themes that emerged from this body of research as they relate to prevention, training, and recruitment efforts in the Air Force.

Lessons Learned for Air Force Prevention, Training, and Recruitment Efforts

Sexual Assault Perpetrators Are a Very Heterogeneous Group

As a whole, the body of literature on sexual assault perpetrators demonstrates that adult sexual assault perpetrators are a heterogeneous group and are diverse in terms of their demographics, background characteristics, and motivations for committing sexual assault. Several researchers have tried to classify them into distinct groups, but there is a lot of overlap between types, and many sexual assault perpetrators commit more nonsexual offenses than sexual offenses.

Implication for Prevention/Intervention

The diversity of sexual assault perpetrators should be stressed in Air Force sexual assault prevention efforts. Although individuals often consider the dynamic between a lone male–stranger rapist and a female victim when thinking about sexual assault, perpetrators in the Air Force likely have diverse background characteristics and motivations for committing sexual assault. To ensure that airmen as well as Air Force leaders are aware of the full range of possible perpetrator types, sexual assault prevention trainings should ensure that scenarios illustrate the heterogeneity of sexual assault perpetrators and include descriptions of the various known motivations, types, and offending patterns among sexual assault perpetrators. This can help dispel any misconceptions that potential perpetrators are easy to identify.

51

Sexual Assault Perpetration Is Likely Influenced by Different Combinations of Factors

As demonstrated in Chapter Three, research has identified many different factors that are correlated with sexual assault perpetration. These factors span a broad range of areas, including developmental factors and family history; individual-level characteristics, such as personality and attitudes/cognitions; and environmental factors, such as peer influences and alcohol consumption. No single identified factor alone, however, has been found to be highly predictive of sexual assault perpetration. Instead, it is likely that a combination of factors influences the probability of committing sexual assault, and these factors interact in different combinations for different people.

Implications for Prevention and Intervention

Research indicates that there are a number of factors related to perpetration that may be susceptible to targeted intervention efforts. These efforts could help decrease the likelihood of sexual assault perpetration, potentially providing the Air Force with the ability to have a more-comprehensive prevention effort addressed at the individual, peer, and community levels.

At the individual level, one of the first steps to prevention would be to screen out recruits likely to commit sexual assault. As noted above, however, factors influencing sexual assault perpetration are complex, and no single identified factor alone has been found to be highly predictive of sexual assault perpetration, making screening using these specific risk factors challenging. Research does find, however, that past perpetration is one of the best predictors of future perpetration. Therefore, the Air Force should continue its current policy to screen out enlisted and officer recruits who have criminal histories of sexual assault perpetration and explore additional mechanisms for identifying past perpetrators, including self-reported engagement in sexual assault.

There are also several studies that demonstrate that certain individual-level attitudes and cognitions are associated with sexual assault perpetration, and these may be malleable through intervention (Anderson and Whiston, 2005). Research points out that rape-myth acceptance, hostility toward women, belief in traditional gender roles, and hypermasculinity are associated with sexual assault perpetration, and these may be targets for prevention efforts.

Currently, some prevention programs that attempt to reduce sexual assault by dispelling rape myths or changing attitudes toward sexual assault are being implemented on university campuses. A meta-analysis that analyzed the effects of these sexual assault prevention programs across multiple studies indicates that the programs are somewhat effective at changing attitudes toward sexual assault; however, there are currently too few studies that examine behavioral outcomes to draw definitive conclusions about whether these types of programs actually decrease the likelihood of committing sexual assault (Anderson and Whiston, 2005).

Another meta-analysis of these programs indicated that the effects of these programs diminish over time; the moderate effects on participants' attitudes observed immediately after the programs were reduced to very small effects within a matter of weeks (Flores and Hartlaub,

1998). Finally, many of the prevention programs on college campuses focus only on one or two factors and lack theoretical or empirical support for their programming elements (DeGue et al., 2014). In the hopes of improving the effectiveness of prevention programs, researchers have recently encouraged future efforts to rely on sound theories, for example, the Confluence Model (DeGue et al., 2014) and/or social psychological theories on belief and behavior change (Paul and Gray, 2011) to design comprehensive prevention programs.

At the peer level, contextual or environmental factors have also been associated with sexual assault perpetration, including peer approval of forced sex, peer pressure for sex, peer sexual aggression, and the use of alcohol. The Air Force should identify opportunities to address some of these contextual factors as part of a comprehensive sexual assault prevention effort. For example, a RAND review of the role of alcohol in sexual assault in the military recommended implementing promising new techniques designed to reduce alcohol misuse (Farris and Hepner, 2014). One such technique involves administering brief behavioral counseling for individuals who score high on alcohol-misuse screenings (Jonas et al., 2012). Other existing efforts that show promise target peers as part of prevention efforts. These bystander-intervention programs encourage peers to intervene in high-risk sexual assault situations, such as stopping a friend from taking a woman who has had too much to drink home or stepping in when a friend's behavior has become sexually aggressive to show peer disapproval for that type of behavior (Banyard, Plante, and Moynihan, 2004).

Finally, a comprehensive prevention effort should not only consider targeting the wide array of known individual- and peer-level factors, but it should also consider community-level factors associated with sexual assault. Findings in Chapter Two on the role of peer influences suggest that it is important to institute social norms that discourage sexual aggression and violence and that promote safety. Some college campuses have recently begun to institute social-norm campaigns that promote messages of peer support for respect and safety and correct misperceptions of support for sexually aggressive behavior (Fabiano et al., 2003). There has yet to be sufficient empirical study of these programs, however, to know whether they reduce the risk of sexual assault.

At the community level, the Air Force also should be sure to target prevention-and-response efforts at the full range of individuals serving in the Air Force, from incoming recruits to individuals within leadership positions. Research suggests that one of the highest-risk periods for sexual assault for university students is the first two years of college, when individuals are exposed to new people and situations (Gross et al., 2006). As incoming Air Force recruits, prevention efforts targeted at these new members may be particularly important. (First-time arrivals to military installations and deployments are likely experiencing similar situations of novelty.) On the other hand, older research on sexual assault risk factors in the military has found that the likelihood of female service members experiencing sexual assault (as measured through self-reporting) was strongly associated with the behaviors of their ranking officers or immediate supervisor; specifically, the odds of reported sexual assault increased when the officers or supervisors permitted sexually demeaning comments or gestures toward female service members (Sadler et al., 2003). Therefore, it is important that sexual assault prevention–training efforts targeting commanders emphasize the importance of their role in fostering a positive environment and reinforcing norms for appropriate behavior and treatment of women. These efforts targeting commanders can also empower them to recognize how their efforts can have an impact on sexual assault prevention.

It should be noted again that these prevention efforts must be accompanied with the understanding that each individual factor plays a very small part in a potential offender's overall risk-factor profile. Therefore, a comprehensive prevention effort, such as that described above, that targets multiple factors at individual, peer, and community levels is likely necessary. Recently, some researchers have called for a focus on multilevel approaches to preventing sexual assault, which include the targeting of peer- and community-level factors associated with sexual assault (Casey and Lindhorst, 2009). Researchers examining the success of campaigns targeted at other forms of unwanted behavior (for example, risky HIV-related sexual behavior or unwanted teen pregnancy) have argued that an important component of these prevention programs has been their comprehensiveness, meaning a focus not only on changing individual-level attitudes and behaviors, but also attitudes within peer networks and social norms within the larger community (Nation et al., 2003).

Implications for Recruitment

The complexity of factors influencing sexual assault perpetration and the multiple pathways that may lead an individual to commit a sexual assault would likely make it difficult to predict whether any one individual is likely to commit sexual assault in the future. In fact, even the most sophisticated and complex theories of offending can account for 30 percent of the variation in sexually aggressive behavior—meaning that it can explain the pathways to different levels of aggression across people. There is a strong potential to misclassify a person as being prone to commit sexual assault who is, in fact, never going to commit a sexual assault. And, conversely, any prediction model will undoubtedly misclassify someone as being low risk, who ends up committing a sexual offense. This would damage the ability of individuals to join the Air Force, and from a Service perspective, this would exclude highly qualified candidates who would perform well in the Air Force and never commit sexual assault.

Sexual Assault Perpetrators Make a Series of Decisions That Lead to Opportunities to Commit Assault

There is scant research available on the behaviors of sexual assault perpetrators outside of serial-stranger perpetrators. Some research examining behavioral patterns in sexual assault perpetration, however, describes a cycle of sexual offending whereby prior to an attack, perpetrators make a series of decisions that leads to an opportunity to commit sexual assault. In addition, the behavior of perpetrators may differ somewhat based on the type of assault—for example, whether the assault is committed by an acquaintance or a stranger or whether alcohol consumption occurs prior to the assault.

Implications for Prevention and Intervention

In the context of sexual assault prevention efforts, there may be points in the decision process in which steps can be taken to prevent or intervene along the pathway to sexual assault. For example, some sexual assault perpetrators may commit sexual assault to compensate for feelings of loneliness or isolation. In the example given in Chapter Three, a perpetrator may consume alcohol to cope with these unpleasant feelings, then go to a bar to continue drinking with intoxicated women, leading to an opportunity to perpetrate sexual assault. Prevention efforts in this example pathway could target coping mechanisms to deal with feelings of isolation or loneliness and strengthen positive peer networks.

In addition, Air Force efforts already underway have the possibility of decreasing risk of sexual assault. For example, Air Force programs devoted to responsible alcohol consumption (including the Air Force's Alcohol and Drug Abuse Prevention and Treatment Program [ADAPT]), bystander-intervention programs, and social activities and facilities that are alternatives to bars and clubs, may each not only serve their overtly defined purpose, but also disrupt decision points that have the potential to lead to sexual assault. It should be stressed that the effectiveness of these programs in reducing incidents of sexual assault has not been empirically evaluated. Rather, we make note of these programs to highlight the possibility that these existing Air Force programs could contribute to a comprehensive strategy to address sexual assault perpetration.

Very Little Is Known About Female, Male-on-Male, and Multiple-Perpetrator Sexual Assault Perpetrators

There is very little research on female perpetrators of sexual assault, and most of it focuses on women who perpetrate against children. Preliminary research indicates that female sexual offenders may experience prior sexual victimization and co-offend with a male partner. There is also very little research on male-on-male sexual assault; however, it appears that there is no single profile and that such perpetrators are a heterogeneous group, with both heterosexual and homosexual perpetrators offending against both heterosexual and homosexual men. It is not known how they differ from men who perpetrate against women. Multiple-perpetrator sexual assaults are also understudied. Preliminary research suggests, however, that it is more likely that offenders use subversion to lure victims into an isolated environment, that more force is used, and that this type of sexual assault is more likely to lead to homicide than single-perpetrator offenses. Social context and psychological processes may play a greater role in multiple-perpetrator sexual assaults than those that involve a single perpetrator.

Implications for Prevention and Intervention

While there is not yet sufficient research evidence on these other types of sexual assault perpetrators to point to any specific areas for developing prevention and intervention efforts, it is important for the Air Force to address these types of sexual assault as part of sexual assault awareness and prevention trainings. Because these types of assault have traditionally been marginalized within society, the Air Force should also prepare trainers to appropriately address jokes or other comments regarding men sexually assaulting men or about women as perpetrators.

Addressing these types of assault will demonstrate to airmen that the Air Force considers each of these forms of sexual assault as serious as one-on-one male-female sexual assault, and that the Air Force intends to detect and hold these perpetrators accountable. This acknowledgment may also prompt individuals who were victims of these types of assaults to come forward and report, particularly if they did not think of themselves as victims of sexual assault, or they feared they would be not taken seriously by the Air Force. As more cases of female, male-on-male, and group sexual assault are reported, the Air Force will be able to learn about the risk factors and behavioral patterns of these types of offenders within the military, which will assist the Air Force in developing targeted prevention efforts.

Future Research

While the significant number of existing studies on the characteristics and behaviors of sexual assault perpetrators provides some important information for the Air Force as it continues its prevention efforts, it is important to note that there are limitations to this research. Furthermore, the design of most sexual assault studies does not provide insight into whether particular factors cause sexual assault perpetration; we only know that these factors are correlated or associated with sexual assault. Considering the complexity of sexual assault perpetration, more research is needed to continue to learn about the characteristics and behaviors of sexual assault perpetrators in the following areas.

Additional Research Is Needed on All Types of Sexual Assault Perpetrators

As evidenced in this report, the vast majority of research has focused on understanding the characteristics and behaviors of individual men who commit sexual assault against a female victim. To date, we know much less about female sexual assault perpetrators, men who assault other men, and multiple-perpetrator sexual assault. Some of the most recent research on sexual assault in the military indicates that at least 4 percent of male service members report experiencing sexual assault during their military careers, usually by male perpetrators (Rock, 2013). Therefore, it is important to gain a deeper understanding of individuals who perpetrate all forms of sexual assault so that prevention efforts can be targeted across all types of assault.

Additional Epidemiological Research Examining Multiple Factors and Their Interaction Over Time Can Provide Additional Insight into Potential Prevention Efforts

As noted, most existing studies of sexual assault perpetrators examine only one or a handful of factors potentially related to sexual assault perpetration. Because we know sexual assault perpetration is likely influenced by a combination of factors, more comprehensive research is needed that considers the wide range of factors that could contribute to sexual assault. This research should be conducted across all types of perpetrators (i.e., male-on-female, male-on-male, female-on-male, and group perpetrators). Further, the current research literature does not follow a representative sample from the general population over time to understand how risk factors lead to sexual assault. Understanding how different factors interact over time and cause sexual assault will require longitudinal research designs that follow large cohorts of people over time. A deeper understanding of how and under what circumstances factors are associated with sexual assault perpetration will assist in determining where to focus sexual assault prevention efforts.

Additional Research Examining the Characteristics and Behaviors of Sexual Assault Perpetrators in the Air Force Is Needed

This literature review focused mainly on the plethora of existing studies examining characteristics and behaviors of sexual assault perpetrators within the general population. To date, only a handful of studies have begun to systematically explore the characteristics and behaviors of military personnel who commit sexual assault during the course of their service (see Turchik and Wilson, 2010, for a review). We do not yet have enough empirical evidence to draw conclusions about the common characteristics and behaviors of sexual assault perpetrators in the military. Much more research with Air Force populations is needed to understand whether the risk factors identified in the community research generalize to the Air Force population and to identify whether there are additional factors specific to the Air Force that should be considered.

Conclusion

The research literature on adult sexual offenders who perpetrate against other adults provides insight into how the Air Force can create a comprehensive prevention strategy. The largest lesson to take away is that sexual offenders are a diverse group of people. Sexual assault perpetration is likely caused by multiple factors and occurs through different developmental pathways. Researchers have identified characteristics associated with perpetration, but according to sophisticated statistical modeling, they have one-third of the variance associated with the sexual aggression. Statistically, this may be considered a good model for predicting something as complex as human behavior, but for applied purposes, use of these factors to identify sexual assault perpetrators will lead to multiple misclassifications. There are some characteristics of male-on-female offenders, however, that may be good targets for prevention, including specific cognitions and attitudes related to violence and gender roles, peer group dynamics, and the use of alcohol. More research is needed to understand the other offender types (e.g., male-on-male, female-on-male, female-on-female, group offenders), how the different offender characteristics influence one another, and how the research findings may or may not apply to the Air Force population.

References

Abbey, Antonia, "Alcohol-Related Sexual Assault: A Common Problem Among College Students," *Journal of Studies on Alcohol*, Vol. 14, 2002, pp. 118–128.

———, "Alcohol's Role in Sexual Violence Perpetration: Theoretical Explanations, Existing Evidence and Future Directions," *Drug and Alcohol Review*, Vol. 30, No. 5, September 2011, pp. 481–489.

Abbey, Antonia, A. Monique Clinton-Sherrod, Pam McAuslan, Tina Zawacki, and Philip O. Buck, "The Relationship Between the Quantity of Alcohol Consumed and the Severity of Sexual Assaults Committed by College Men," *Journal of Interpersonal Violence*, Vol. 18, No. 7, July 2003, pp. 813–833.

Abbey, Antonia, and Pam McAuslan, "A Longitudinal Examination of Male College Students' Perpetration of Sexual Assault," *Journal of Consulting and Clinical Psychology*, Vol. 72, No. 5, October 2004, pp. 747–756.

Abbey, Antonia, Pam McAuslan, and Lisa Thomson Ross, "Sexual Assault Perpetration by College Men: The Role of Alcohol, Misperception of Sexual Intent, and Sexual Beliefs and Experiences," *Journal of Social and Clinical Psychology*, Vol. 17, No. 1, January 1998, pp. 167–195.

Abbey, Antonia, Pam McAusland, Tina Zawacki, A. Monique Clinton, and Phillip O. Buck, "Attitudinal, Experiential, and Situational Predictors of Sexual Assault Perpetration," *Journal of Interpersonal Violence*, Vol. 16, No. 8, August 2001, pp. 784–807.

Abbey, Antonia, Michele R. Parkhill, Renee BeShears, A. Monique Clinton-Sherrod, and Tina Zawacki, "Cross-Sectional Predictors of Sexual Assault Perpetration in a Community Sample of Single African American and Caucasian Men," *Aggressive Behavior*, Vol. 32, No. 1, February 2006, pp. 54–67.

Abbey, Antonia, Michele R. Parkhill, A. Monique Clinton-Sherrod, and Tina Zawacki, "A Comparison of Men Who Committed Different Types of Sexual Assault in a Community Sample," *Journal of Interpersonal Violence*, Vol. 22, No. 12, 2007, pp. 1567–1580.

Abbey, Antonia, Tina Zawacki, and Phillip O. Buck, "The Effects of Past Sexual Assault Perpetration and Alcohol Consumption on Men's Reactions to Women's Mixed Signals," *Journal of Social and Clinical Psychology*, Vol. 24, No. 2, March 2005, pp. 129–155.

Adams-Curtis, Leah E., and Gordon B. Forbes, "College Women's Experiences of Sexual Coercion: A Review of Cultural, Perpetrator, Victim, and Situational Variables," *Trauma, Violence, and Abuse*, Vol. 5, No. 2, April 2004, pp. 9–22.

Almond, Louise, Michelle A. McManus, and Lydia Ward, "Male-on-Male Sexual Assaults: An Analysis of Crime Scene Actions," *Journal of Interpersonal Violence*, November 2013, pp. 1–18.

Anderson, Eric, Mark McCormack, and Harry Lee, "Male Team Sport Hazing Initiations in a Culture of Decreasing Homohysteria," *Journal of Adolescent Research*, Vol. 27, No. 4, July 2012, pp. 427–448.

Anderson, Linda A., and Susan C. Whiston, "Sexual Assault Education Programs: A Meta-Analytic Examination of Their Effectiveness," *Psychology of Women Quarterly*, Vol. 29, No. 4, December 2005, pp. 374–388.

Anderson, Peter B., Anthony Kontos, Holly Tanigoshi, and Cindy Struckman-Johnson, "An Examination of Sexual Strategies Used by Urban Southern and Rural Midwestern University Women," *The Journal of Sex Research*, Vol. 42, No. 4, November 2005, pp. 335–341.

Anderson, Peter B., and Maria Newton, "Predicting the Use of Sexual Initiation Tactics in a Sample of College Women," *Electronic Journal of Human Sexuality*, Vol. 7, May 2004, pp. 1–15.

Bachman, Ronet, "The Factors Related to Rape Reporting Behavior and Arrest New Evidence from the National Crime Victimization Survey," *Criminal Justice and Behavior*, Vol. 25, No. 1, March 1998, pp. 8–29.

Bandura, Albert, Bill Underwood, and Michael E. Fromson, "Disinhibition of Aggression Through Diffusion of Responsibility and Dehumanization of Victims," *Journal of Research in Personality*, Vol. 9, December 1975, pp. 25–269.

Banyard, Victoria L., Elizabethe G. Plante, and Mary M. Moynihan, "Bystander Education: Bringing a Broader Community Perspective to Sexual Violence Prevention," *Journal of Community Psychology*, Vol. 32, No. 1, January 2004, pp. 6–79.

Baumeister, Roy F., and Mark R. Leary, "The Need to Belong: Desire for Interpersonal Attachments as a Fundamental Human Motivation," *Psychological Bulletin*, Vol. 117, No. 3, May 1995, pp. 497–529.

Beauregard, Eric, and Benoit Leclerc, "An Application of the Rational Choice Approach to the Offending Process of Sex Offenders: A Closer Look at the Decision-Making," *Sexual Abuse: A Journal of Research and Treatment*, Vol. 19, No. 2, June 2007, pp. 115–133.

Beauregard, Eric, Jean Proulx, Kim Rossmo, Benoit Leclerc, and Jean-Francois Allaire, "Script Analysis of the Hunting Process of Serial Sex Offenders," *Criminal Justice and Behavior*, Vol. 34, No. 8, August 2007, pp. 1069–1084.

Black, Michele C., Kathleen C. Basile, Matthew J. Breiding, Sharon G. Smith, Mikel L. Walters, Melissa T. Merrick, Jieru Chen, and M. R. Stevens, *National Intimate Partner and Sexual*

Violence Survey: 2010 Summary Report, Atlanta, Ga.: National Center for Injury Prevention and Control, Centers for Disease Control and Prevention, 2011.

Black, Michele C., and Melissa T. Merrick, *Prevalence of Intimate Partner Violence, Sexual Violence, and Stalking Among Active Duty Women and Wives of Active Duty Men— Comparisons with Women in the U.S. General Population, 2010*, Atlanta, Ga.: National Center for Injury Prevention and Control, Centers for Disease Control and Prevention, 2013.

Bostock, Deborah J., and James G. Daley, "Lifetime and Current Sexual Assault and Harassment Victimization Rates of Active-Duty United State Air Force Women," *Violence Against Women*, Vol. 13, No. 9, September 2007, pp. 927–944.

Bourgois, Philippe, "In Search of Masculinity: Violence, Respect, and Sexuality Among Puerto Rican Crack Dealers in East Harlem," *British Journal of Criminology*, Vol. 36, No. 3, January 1996, pp. 412–427.

Bownes, Ian T., Ethan C. O'Gorman, and Angela Sayers, "Rape—A Comparison of Stranger and Acquaintance Assaults," *Medicine, Science and the Law*, Vol. 31, No. 2, May 1991, pp. 102–109.

Brecklin, Leanne R., and Sarah E. Ullman, "The Role of Offender Alcohol Use in Rape Attacks: An Analysis of National Crime Victimization Survey Data," *Journal of Interpersonal Violence*, Vol. 16, No. 1, January 2001, pp. 3–21.

Breiding, Matthew J., Charon G. Smith, Kathleen C. Basile, Mikel L. Walters, Jieru Chen, and Melissa T. Merrick, "Prevalence and Characteristics of Sexual Violence, Stalking, and Intimate Partner Violence Victimization—National Intimate Partner and Sexual Violence Survey, United States, 2011," *Morbidity and Mortality Weekly Report (MMWR)*, Vol. 63, No. 8, September 2014, pp. 1–19.

Burt, Martha R., "Cultural Myths and Supports for Rape," *Journal of Personality and Social Psychology*, Vol. 38, No. 2, 1980, pp. 217–230.

Butcher, James Neal, *Minnesota Multiphasic Personality Inventory®-2: Manual for Administration, Scoring, and Interpretation*, Minneapolis, Minn.: University of Minnesota Press, 2001.

Calhoun, Karen S., Jeffrey A. Bernat, Gretchen A. Clum, and Cynthia L. Frame, "Sexual Coercion and Attraction to Sexual Aggression in a Community Sample of Young Men," *Journal of Interpersonal Violence*, Vol. 12, No. 3, June 1997, pp. 392–406.

Capaldi, Deborah M., Thomas J. Dishion, Mike Stoolmiller, and Karen Yoerger, "Aggression Toward Female Partners by At-Risk Young Men: The Contribution of Male Adolescent Friendships," *Developmental Psychology*, Vol. 37, No. 1, January 2001, pp. 61–73.

Carr, Joetta L., and Karen M. VanDeusen, "Risk Factors for Male Sexual Aggression on College Campuses," *Journal of Family Violence*, Vol. 19, No. 5, October 2004, pp. 279–289.

Casey, Erin A., and Taryn P. Lindhorst, "Toward a Multilevel, Ecological Approach to the Primary Prevention of Sexual Assault Prevention in Peer and Community Contexts," *Trauma, Violence, and Abuse*, Vol. 10, No. 2, April 2009, pp. 91–114.

Chambers, Jemma C., Miranda A. H. Horvath, and Liz Kelly, "A Typology of Multiple Perpetrator Rape," *Criminal Justice and Behavior*, Vol. 37, No. 10, October 2010, pp. 1114–1139.

Check, James Victor Patrick, *The Hostility Toward Women Scale*, dissertation, University of Manitoba, Ann Arbor, Mich.: Dissertation Abstracts International, Vol. 45, 3993, 1985.

Christopher, F. Scott, Mary Madura, and Lori Weaver, "Premarital Sexual Aggressors: A Multivariate Analysis of Social, Relational, and Individual Variables," *Journal of Marriage and the Family*, Vol. 60, No. 1, 1998, pp. 56–69.

da Silva, Teresa, Jessica Woodhams, and Leigh Harkins, "Heterogeneity Within Multiple Perpetrator Rapes: A National Comparison of Lone, Duo, and 3+ Perpetrator Rapes," *Sexual Abuse*, 2013, pp. 1–20.

Davis, Joanne L., Patricia A. Petretic-Jackson, and Ling Ting, "Intimacy Dysfunction and Trauma Symptomatology: Long-Term Correlates of Different Types of Child Abuse," *Journal of Traumatic Stress*, Vol. 14, No. 1, January 2001, pp. 63–79.

Davis, Karen M., and Robert P. Archer, "A Critical Review of Objective Personality Inventories with Sex Offenders," *Journal of Clinical Psychology*, Vol. 66, No. 12, 2010, pp. 1254–1280.

Davis, Kelly Cue, Trevor Schraufnagel, William George, and Jeanette Norris, "The Use of Alcohol and Condoms During Sexual Assault," *American Journal of Men's Heath*, Vol. 2, No. 3, September 2008, pp. 1–10.

DeGue, Sarah, and David DiLillo, "'You Would If You Loved Me'": Toward an Improved Conceptual and Etiological Understanding of Nonphysical Male Sexual Coercion," *Aggression and Violent Behavior*, Vol. 10, No. 4, May/June 2005, pp. 513–532.

DeGue, Sarah, David DiLillo, and Mario Scalora, "Are All Perpetrators Alike? Comparing Risk Factors for Sexual Coercion and Aggression," *Sexual Abuse: A Journal of Research and Treatment*, Vol. 22, No. 4, 2010, pp. 402–426.

DeGue, Sarah, Linda Anne Valle, Melissa K. Holt, Greta M. Massetti, Jennifer L. Matjasko, and Andra Teten Tharp, "A Systematic Review of Primary Prevention Strategies for Sexual Violence Perpetration," *Aggression and Violent Behavior*, Vol. 19, No. 4, July/August 2014, pp. 346–362.

DeKeseredy, Walter S., and Katharine Kelly, "Sexual Abuse in Canadian University and College Dating Relationships: The Contribution of Male Peer Support," *Journal of Family Violence*, Vol. 10, No. 1, 1995, pp. 41–53.

Fabiano, Patricia M., Wesley Perkins, Alan Berkowitz, Jeff Linkenbach, and Christopher Stark, "Engaging Men as Social Justice Allies in Ending Violence Against Women: Evidence for a Social Norms Approach," *Journal of American College Health*, Vol. 52, No. 3, 2003, pp. 105–112.

Farris, Coreen, and Kimberly A. Hepner, *Targeting Alcohol Use: A Promising Strategy for Reducing Military Sexual Assaults?* Santa Monica, Calif.: RAND Corporation, RR-538-OSD, 2014. As of September 3, 2015: http://www.rand.org/pubs/research_reports/RR538.html

Farris, Coreen, Teresa A. Treat, Richard J. Viken, and Richard M. McFall, "Perceptual Mechanisms That Characterize Gender Differences in Decoding Women's Sexual Intent," *Psychological Science*, Vol. 19, No. 4, 2008a, pp. 348–354.

———, "Sexual Coercion and the Misperception of Sexual Intent," *Clinical Psychology Review*, Vol. 28, 2008b, pp. 48–66.

Federal Bureau of Investigation, *Crime in the United States, 2005: Uniform Crime Reports*, Washington, D.C.: United States Department of Justice, 2006. As of September 9, 2015: https://www2.fbi.gov/ucr/05cius

Feldhaus, Kim M., Debra Houry, and Robin Kaminsky, "Lifetime Sexual Assault Prevalence Rates and Reporting Practices in an Emergency Department Population," *Annals of Emergency Medicine*, Vol. 36, No. 1, July 2000, pp. 23–27.

Felson, Richard B., Steven F. Messner, and Anthony Hoskin, "The Victim-Offender Relationship and Calling Police in Assaults," *Criminology*, Vol. 37, No. 4, November 1999, pp. 931–948.

Ferguson, Christopher J., and D. Cricket Meehan, "An Analysis of Females Convicted of Sex Crimes in the State of Florida," *Journal of Child Sexual Abuse*, Vol. 14, No. 1, 2005, pp. 75–89.

Fernandez, Yolanda M., and W. L. Marshall, "Victim Empathy, Social Self-Esteem, and Psychopathy in Rapists," *Sexual Abuse: A Journal of Research and Treatment*, Vol. 15, No. 1, January 2003, pp. 11–26.

Festinger, Leon, "A Theory of Social Comparison Processes," *Human Relations*, Vol. 7, No. 2, May 1954, pp. 117–140.

Fisher, Terri D., and Andrew S. Walters, "Variables in Addition to Gender That Help to Explain Differences in Perceived Sexual Interest," *Psychology of Men and Masculinity*, Vol. 4, No. 2, 2003, pp. 154–162.

Fiske, Susan T., *Social Beings: Core Motives in Social Psychology*, Hoboken, N.J.: John Wiley and Sons, 2004.

Flores, Stephen A., and Mark G. Hartlaub, "Reducing Rape-Myth Acceptance in Male College Students: A Meta-Analysis of Intervention Studies," *Journal of College Student Development*, Vol. 39, No. 5, September/October 1998, pp. 438–448.

Forbes, Gordon B., Leah E. Adams-Curtis, and Kay B. White, "First- and Second-Generation Measures of Sexism, Rape Myths and Related Beliefs, and Hostility Toward Women: Their Interrelationships and Association with College Students' Experiences with Dating Aggression and Sexual Coercion," *Violence Against Women*, Vol. 10, No. 3, 2004, pp. 236–261.

Franklin, Cortney A., Leana Allen Bouffard, and Travis C. Pratt, "Sexual Assault on the College Campus Fraternity Affiliation, Male Peer Support, and Low Self-Control," *Criminal Justice and Behavior*, Vol. 39, No. 11, 2012, pp. 1457–1480.

Franklin, Karen, "Masculinity, Status, and Power: Implicit Messages in Western Media Discourse on High-Profile Cases of Multiple Perpetrator Rape," in Miranda A. H. Horvath and Jessica Woodhams, eds., *Handbook on the Study of Multiple Perpetrator Rape: A Multidisciplinary Response to an International Problem*, New York: Routledge, 2013, pp. 37–66.

Frazier, Patricia A, "A Comparative Study of Male and Female Rape Victims Seen at a Hospital-Based Rape Crisis Program," *Journal of Interpersonal Violence*, Vol. 8, No. 1, 1993, pp. 64–76.

Fromuth, Mary Ellen, and Victoria E. Conn, "Hidden Perpetrators: Sexual Molestation in a Nonclinical Sample of College Women," *Journal of Interpersonal Violence*, Vol. 12, No. 3, 1997, pp. 456–465.

Gartner, Rosemary, and Ross Macmillan, "Effect of Victim-Offender Relationship on Reporting Crimes of Violence Against Women," *The Canadian Journal of Criminology*, Vol. 37, No. 3, 1995, pp. 393–429.

Geer, James H., Laura A. Estupinan, and Gina M. Manguno-Mire, "Empathy, Social Skills, and Other Relevant Cognitive Processes in Rapists and Child Molesters," *Aggression and Violent Behavior*, Vol. 5, No. 1, January 2000, pp. 99–126.

Gidycz, Christine A., Catherine Loh, Traci Lobo, Cindy Rich, Steven Jay Lynn, and Joanna Pashdag, "Reciprocal Relationships Among Alcohol Use, Risk Perception, and Sexual

Victimization: A Prospective Analysis," *Journal of American College Health*, Vol. 56, No. 1, 2007, pp. 5–14.

Gold, Steven R., Jim Fultz, Cathy H. Burke, Andrew G. Prisco, and John A. Willett, "Vicarious Emotional Responses of Macho College Males," *Journal of Interpersonal Violence*, Vol. 7, No. 2, June 1992, pp. 165–174.

Greene, Patricia Logan, and Kelly Cue Davis, "Latent Profiles of Risk Among a Community Sample of Men: Implications for Sexual Aggression," *Journal of Interpersonal Violence*, Vol. 26, No. 7, May 2011, pp. 1463–1477.

Grier, Priscilla E., "Cognitive Problem-Solving Skills in Antisocial Rapists," *Criminal Justice and Behavior*, Vol. 15, No. 4, December 1988, pp. 501–514.

Gross, Alan M., Andrea Winslett, Miguel Roberts, and Carol L. Gohm, "An Examination of Sexual Violence Against College Women," *Violence Against Women*, Vol. 12, No. 3, March 2006, pp. 288–300.

Grover, Brianna Leigh, "The Utility of MMPI-2 Scores with a Correctional Population and Convicted Sex Offenders," *Psychology*, Vol. 2, No. 6, 2011, pp. 638–642.

Gudjonsson, Gisli H., and Jon F. Sigurdsson, "Differences and Similarities Between Violent Offenders and Sex Offenders," *Child Abuse and Neglect*, Vol. 24, No. 3, March 2000, pp. 363–372.

Hall, Gordon C. Nagayama, Stanley Sue, David S. Narang, and Roy S. Lilly, "Culture-Specific Models of Men's Sexual Aggression: Intra- and Interpersonal Determinants," *Cultural Diversity and Ethnic Minority Psychology*, Vol. 6, No. 3, August 2000, pp. 252–267.

Hall, Gordon C. Nagayama, Andra L. Teten, David S. DeGarmo, Stanley Sue, and Kari A. Stephens, "Ethnicity, Culture, and Sexual Aggression: Risk and Protective Factors," *Journal of Consulting and Clinical Psychology*, Vol. 73, No. 5, 2005, pp. 830–840.

Hanson, Robert Karl, and Monique T. Bussière, "Predicting Relapse: A Meta-Analysis of Sexual Offender Recidivism Studies," *Journal of Consulting and Clinical Psychology*, Vol. 66, No. 2, 1998, pp. 348–362.

Hanson, Robert Karl, and Kelly E. Morton-Bourgon, "The Characteristics of Persistent Sexual Offenders: A Meta-Analysis of Recidivism Studies," *Journal of Consulting and Clinical Psychology*, Vol. 73, No. 5, December 2005, pp. 1154–1163.

Hanson, Robert Karl, and S. Slater, "Sexual Victimization in the History of Sexual Abusers: A Review," *Annals of Sex Research*, Vol. 1, No. 4, 1988, pp. 485–499.

Hanson, Robert Karl, and David Thornton, *Static 99: Improving Actuarial Risk Assessments for Sex Offenders*, Vol. 2, Ottawa, Canada: The Department of the Solicitor General of Canada, Ottawa, and Her Majesty's Prison Service, London, 1999.

Harkins, Leigh, and Louise Dixon, "Sexual Offending in Groups," *Aggression and Violent Behavior*, Vol. 15, No. 2, 2010, pp. 87–99.

Hauffe, Sarah, and Louise Porter, "An Interpersonal Comparison of Lone and Group Rape Offences," *Psychology Crime and Law*, Vol. 15, No. 5, June 2009, pp. 469–491.

Hickson, Ford C. I., Peter M. Davies, Andrew J. Hunt, Peter Weatherburn, Thomas J. McManus, and Anthony P. M. Coxon, "Gay Men as Victims of Nonconsensual Sex," *Archives of Sexual Behavior*, Vol. 23, No. 3, 1994, pp. 281–294.

Hodge, Samantha, and David Canter, "Victims and Perpetrators of Male Sexual Assault," *Journal of Interpersonal Violence*, Vol. 13, No. 2, 1998, pp. 222–239.

Horvath, Miranda Angel Helena, and Liz Kelly, "Multiple Perpetrator Rape: Naming an Offence and Initial Research Findings," *Journal of Sexual Aggression,* Vol. 15, No. 1, 2009, pp. 83–96.

Hoyt, Tim, Jennifer Klosterman Rielage, and Lauren F. Williams, "Military Sexual Trauma in Men: A Review of Reported Rates," *Journal of Trauma and Dissociation*, Vol. 12, No. 3, 2011, pp. 244–260.

Humphrey, Stephen E., and Arnold S. Kahn, "Fraternities, Athletic Teams, and Rape," *Journal of Interpersonal Violence*, Vol. 15, No. 12, 2000, pp. 1313–1320.

Isely, Paul J., and David Gehrenbeck-Shim, "Sexual Assault of Men in the Community," *Journal of Community Psychology*, Vol. 25, No. 2, 1997, pp. 159–166.

Jespersen, Ashley F., Martin L. Lalumière, and Michael C. Seto, "Sexual Abuse History Among Adult Sex Offenders and Non-Sex Offenders: A Meta-Analysis," *Child Abuse and Neglect*, Vol. 33, 2009, pp. 179–192.

Jewkes, Rachel, *Rape Perpetration: A Review*, Pretoria, South Africa: Sexual Violence Research Initiative, 2012.

Johansson-Love, Jill, and William Fremouw, "A Critique of the Female Sexual Perpetrator Research," *Aggression and Violent Behavior*, Vol. 11, 2006, pp. 12–26.

Jonas, Daniel E., James C. Garbutt, Halle R. Amick, Janice M. Brown, Kimberly A. Brownley, Carol L. Council, Anthony J. Viera, Tania M. Wilkins, Cody J. Schwartz, Emily M. Richmond, John Yeatts, Mammeka Swinson Evans, Sally D. Wood, and Russell P. Harris, "Behavioral Counseling After Screening for Alcohol Misuse in Primary Care: A Systematic

Review and Meta-Analysis for the U.S. Preventive Services Task Force," *Annals of Internal Medicine*, Vol. 157, No. 9, November 6, 2012, pp. 645–654.

Jones, Jeffrey S., Barbara N. Wynn, Boyd Kroeze, Chris Dunnuck, and Linda Rossman, "Comparison of Sexual Assaults by Strangers Versus Known Assailants in a Community-Based Population," *American Journal of Emergency Medicine*, Vol. 22, No. 6, October 2004, pp. 454–459.

Kanin, Eugene J., "Date Rapists: Differential Sexual Socialization and Relative Deprivation," *Archives of Sexual Behavior*, Vol. 14, No. 3, 1985, pp. 219–231.

Kaufman, Joan, and Edward Zigler, "Do Abused Children Become Abusive Parents?" *American Journal of Orthopsychiatry*, Vol. 57, No. 2, April 1987, pp. 186–192.

Kaysen, Debra, Tiara M. Dillworth, Tracy Simpson, Angela Waldrop, Mary E. Larimer, and Patricia A. Resick, "Domestic Violence and Alcohol Use: Trauma-Related Symptoms and Motives for Drinking," *Addictive Behaviors*, Vol. 32, No. 6, June 2007, pp. 1272–1283.

Kingree, Jeffrey B., and Martie P. Thompson, "Fraternity Membership and Sexual Aggression: An Examination of Mediators of the Association," *Journal of American College Health*, Vol. 61, No. 4, 2013, pp. 213–221.

Kirby, Sandra L., and Glen Wintrup, "Running the Gauntlet: An Examination of Initiation/Hazing and Sexual Abuse in Sport," *Journal of Sexual Aggression*, Vol. 8, No. 2, 2002, pp. 49–68.

Knight, Raymond A., and Judith E. Sims-Knight, "The Developmental Antecedents of Sexual Coercion Against Women: Testing Alternative Hypotheses with Structural Equation Modeling," *Annals of the New York Academy of Sciences*, Vol. 989, 2003, pp. 72–85.

Koss, Mary P., "Rape: Scope, Impact, Interventions, and Public Policy Responses," *American Psychologist*, Vol. 48, No. 10, 1993 pp. 1062–1069.

Koss, Mary P., Thomas E. Dinero, Cynthia A. Seibel, and Susan L. Cox, "Stranger and Acquaintance Rape: Are There Differences in the Victim's Experience?" *Psychology of Women Quarterly*, Vol. 12, No. 1, 1988, pp. 1–24.

Krahé, Barbara, Renate Scheinberger-Olwig, and Stephan Schütze, "Risk Factors of Sexual Aggression and Victimization Among Homosexual Men," *Journal of Applied Social Psychology*, Vol. 31, No. 7, 2001, pp. 1385–1408.

Langevin, R., P. Wright, and L. Handy, "Empathy, Assertiveness, Aggressiveness, and Defensiveness Among Sex Offenders," *Annals of Sex Research*, Vol. 1, 1988, pp. 533–547.

Lawyer, Steven, Heidi Resnick, Von Bakanic, Tracy Burkett, and Dean Kilpatrick, "Forcible, Drug-Facilitated, and Incapacitated Rape and Sexual Assault Among Undergraduate Women," *Journal of American College Health*, Vol. 58, No. 5, 2010, pp. 453–460.

Lee, Joseph K. P., Henry J. Jackson, Pip Pattison, and Tony Ward, "Developmental Risk Factors for Sexual Offending," *Child Abuse and Neglect*, Vol. 26, No. 1, 2002, pp. 73–92.

Leeb, R. T., L. J. Paulozzi, C. Melanson, T. R. Simon, and I. Arias, *Child Maltreatment Surveillance: Uniform Definitions for Public Health and Recommended Data Elements*, version 1.0, Atlanta, Ga.: National Center for Injury Prevention and Control, Centers for Disease Control and Prevention, January 2008.

Lewis, Catherine F., and Charlotte R. Stanley, "Women Accused of Sexual Offenses," *Behavioral Sciences and the Law*, Vol. 18, No. 1, January/February 2000, pp. 73–81.

Lilly, J. Robert, "Counterblast: Soldiers and Rape: The Other Band of Brothers," *The Howard Journal*, Vol. 46, No. 1, February 2007, pp. 72–75.

Locke, Benjamin D., and James R. Mahalik, "Examining Masculinity Norms, Problem Drinking, and Athletic Involvement as Predictors of Sexual Aggression in College Men," *Journal of Counseling Psychology*, Vol. 52, No. 3, July 2005, pp. 279–283.

Loh, Catherine, and Christine A. Gidycz, "A Prospective Analysis of the Relationship Between Childhood Sexual Victimization and Perpetration of Dating Violence and Sexual Assault in Adulthood," *Journal of Interpersonal Violence*, Vol. 21, No. 6, 2006, pp. 732–749.

Loh, Catherine, Christine A. Gidycz, Tracy R. Lobo, and Rohini Luthra, "A Prospective Analysis of Sexual Assault Perpetration: Risk Factors Related to Perpetrator Characteristics," *Journal of Interpersonal Violence*, Vol. 20, No. 10, October 2005, pp. 1325–1348.

Lonsway, Kimberly A., and Louise F. Fitzgerald, "Attitudinal Antecedents of Rape Myth Acceptance: A Theoretical and Empirical Reexamination," *Journal of Personality and Social Psychology*, Vol. 68, No. 4, 1995, pp. 704–711.

Lyn, Tamara S., and David L. Burton, "Attachment, Anger, and Anxiety of Male Sexual Offenders," *Journal of Sexual Aggression*, Vol. 11, No. 2, 2005, pp. 127–137.

Lyndon, Amy E., Jacquelyn W. White, and Kelly M. Kadlec, "Manipulation and Force as Sexual Coercion Tactics: Conceptual and Empirical Differences," *Aggressive Behavior*, Vol. 33, No. 4, July/August 2007, pp. 291–303.

Mackie, Diane, "Social Identification Effects in Group Polarization," *Journal of Personality and Social Psychology*, Vol. 50, No. 4, April 1986, pp. 720–728.

Malamuth, Neil M., "The Confluence Model of Sexual Aggression: Feminist and Evolutionary Perspectives," in David M. Buss and Neil M. Malamuth, eds., *Sex, Power, Conflict:*

Evolutionary and Feminist Perspectives, New York: Oxford University Press, 1996, pp. 269–295.

Malamuth, Neil M., Daniel Linz, Christopher L. Heavey, Gordon Barnes, and Michele Acker, "Using the Confluence Model of Sexual Aggression to Predict Men's Conflict with Women: A Ten-Year Follow-Up Study," *Journal of Personality and Social Psychology*, Vol. 69, No. 2, 1995, pp. 353–369.

Malamuth, Neil M., Robert J. Sockloskie, Mary P. Koss, and J. S. Tanaka, "Characteristics of Aggressors Against Women: Testing a Model Using a National Sample of College Students," *Journal of Consulting and Clinical Psychology*, Vol. 59, No. 5, 1991, pp. 670–681.

Marshall, William L., Dana Anderson, Yolanda Fernandez, and Rachel Mulloy, *Cognitive Behavioural Treatment of Sexual Offenders*, Chichester, U.K.: John Wiley, 1999.

Marshall, William L., and H. E. Barbaree, "An Integrated Theory of the Etiology of Sexual Offending," in William L. Marshall, D. R. Laws, and Howard E. Barbaree, eds., *Handbook of Sexual Assault*, New York: Springer U.S., 1990.

Marshall, William L., S. M. Hudson, R. Jones, and Yolanda Maria Fernandez, "Empathy in Sex Offenders," *Clinical Psychology Review*, Vol. 15, No. 2, 1995, pp. 99–113.

Martin, Patricia Yancey, and Robert A. Hummer, "Fraternities and Rape on Campus," *Gender and Society*, Vol. 3, No. 4, December 1989, pp. 457–473.

Marx, Brian P., Alan M. Gross, and Henry E. Adams, "The Effect of Alcohol on the Responses of Sexually Coercive and Noncoercive Men to an Experimental Rape Analogue, *Sexual Abuse: A Journal of Research and Treatment*, Vol. 11, No. 2 1999, pp. 131–145.

Mathews, Ruth, Jane Kinder Matthews, and Kathleen Speltz, *Female Sexual Offenders: An Exploratory Study*, Brandon, Vt.: Safer Society Press, 1989.

McCormack, Julie, Stephen M. Hudson, and Tony Ward, "Sexual Offenders' Perceptions of Their Early Interpersonal Relationships: An Attachment Perspective," *Journal of Sex Research*, Vol. 39, No. 2, May 2002, pp. 85–93.

McFall, R. M.,"The Enhancement of Social Skills," in William L. Marshall, D. R. Laws, and Howard E. Barbaree, eds., *Handbook of Sexual Assault*, New York: Springer U.S., 1990, pp. 311–330.

McGrath, Mary, Steven Cann, and Robert Konopasky, "New Measures of Defensiveness, Empathy, and Cognitive Distortions for Sexual Offenders Against Children," *Sexual Abuse: A Journal of Research and Treatment*, Vol. 10, No. 1, 1998, pp. 25–36.

McWhorter, Stephanie K., Valerie A. Stander, Lex L. Merrill, Cynthia J. Thomsen, and Joel S. Milner, "Reports of Rape Reperpetration by Newly Enlisted Male Navy Personnel," *Violence and Victims*, Vol. 24, No. 2, 2009, pp. 204–218.

Ménard, Kim S., Gordon C. Nagayama Hall, Amber H. Phung, Marian F. Erian Ghebrial, and Lynette Martin, "Gender Differences in Sexual Harassment and Coercion in College Students: Developmental, Individual, and Situational Determinants," *Journal of Interpersonal Violence*, Vol. 18, No. 10, October 2003, pp. 1222–1239.

Merrill, Lex L., Cynthia J. Thomsen, Steven R. Gold, and Joel S. Milner, "Childhood Abuse and Premilitary Sexual Assault in Male Navy Recruits," *Journal of Consulting and Clinical Psychology*, Vol. 69, No. 2, 2001, pp. 252–261.

Mohler-Kuo, Meichun, George W. Dowdall, Mary P. Koss, and Henry Wechsler, "Correlates of Rape While Intoxicated in a National Sample of College Women," *Journal of Studies on Alcohol*, Vol. 65, January 2004, pp. 37–45.

Morey, Leslie C., *Personality Assessment Inventory (PAI)*, Lutz, Fla.: PAR, 1991.

Morgan, Louise, Bernadette Brittain, and Jan Welch, "Multiple Perpetrator Sexual Assault: How Does It Differ from Assault by a Single Perpetrator?" *Journal of Interpersonal Violence*, Vol. 27, No. 12, 2012, pp. 2415–2436.

Morral, Andrew R., Kristie L. Gore, Terry L. Schell, Barbara Bicksler, Coreen Farris, Bonnie Ghosh-Dastidar, Lisa H. Jaycox, Dean Kilpatrick, Stephan Kistler, Amy Street, Terri Tanielian, and Kayla M. Williams, *Sexual Assault and Sexual Harassment in the U.S. Military:* Vol. 2, *Estimates for Department of Defense Service Members from the 2014 RAND Military Workplace Study*, Santa Monica, Calif.: RAND Corporation, RR-870/2-OSD, 2015. As of September 4, 2015:
http://www.rand.org/pubs/research_reports/RR870z2.html

Mosher, Donald L., and Ronald D. Anderson, "Macho Personality, Sexual Aggression, and Reactions to Guided Imagery of Realistic Rape," *Journal of Research in Personality*, Vol. 20, No. 1, 1986, pp. 77–94.

Mosher, Donald L., and Mark Sirkin, "Measuring a Macho Personality Constellation," *Journal of Research in Personality*, Vol. 18, No. 2, 1984, pp. 150–163.

Muller, Robert T., and Terry Diamond, "Father and Mother Physical Abuse and Child Aggressive Behaviour in Two Generations," *Canadian Journal of Behavioural Science*, Vol. 31, No. 4, 1999, pp. 221–228.

Murdoch, Maureen, John Barron Pryor, Melissa Anderson Polusny, and Gary Dean Gackstetter, "Functioning and Psychiatric Symptoms Among Military Men and Women Exposed to Sexual Stressors," *Military Medicine*, Vol. 172, No. 7, 2007, pp. 718–725.

Murnen, Sarah K., Carrie Wright, and Gretchen Kaluzny, "If 'Boys Will Be Boys,' Then Girls Will Be Victims? A Meta-Analytic Review of the Research That Relates Masculine Ideology to Sexual Aggression," *Sex Roles*, Vol. 46, Nos. 11/12, June 2002, pp. 359–375.

Murphy, William D., "Assessment and Modification of Cognitive Distortions in Sex Offenders," in William L. Marshall, D. R. Laws, and Howard E. Barbaree, eds., *Handbook of Sexual Assault*, New York: Springer U.S., 1990, pp. 331–342.

Myers, David G., "Polarizing Effects of Social Comparison," *Journal of Experimental Social Psychology*, Vol. 14, No. 6, 1978, pp. 554–563.

Nathan, Pamela, and Tony Ward, "Female Sex Offenders: Clinical and Demographic Features," *Journal of Sexual Aggression*, Vol. 8, No. 1, 2002, pp. 5–21.

Nation, Maury, Cindy Crusto, Abraham Wandersman, Karol L. Kumpfer, Diana Seybolt, Erin Morrissey-Kane, and Katrina Davino, "What Works in Prevention: Principles of Effective Prevention Programs," *American Psychologist*, Vol. 58, No. 6/7, June/July 2003, pp. 449–456.

Olver, Mark E., Stephen C. P. Wong, Terry Nicholaichuk, and Audrey Gordon, "The Validity and Reliability of the Violence Risk Scale-Sexual Offender Version: Assessing Sex Offender Risk and Evaluating Therapeutic Change," *Psychological Assessment*, Vol. 19, No. 3, September 2007, pp. 318–329.

Overholser, James C., and Steven Beck, "Multimethod Assessment of Rapists, Child Molesters, and Three Control Groups on Behavioral and Psychological Measures," *Journal of Consulting and Clinical Psychology*, Vol. 54, No. 5, 1986, pp. 682–687.

Parkhill, Michele R., and Antonia Abbey, "Does Alcohol Contribute to the Confluence Model of Sexual Assault Perpetration?" *Journal of Social and Clinical Psychology*, Vol. 27, No. 6, 2008, pp. 529–554.

Parkhill, Michele R., Antonia Abbey, and Angela J. Jacques-Tiura, "How Do Sexual Assault Characteristics Vary as a Function of Perpetrators' Level of Intoxication?" *Addictive Behaviors*, Vol. 34, No. 3, 2009, pp. 331–333.

Parrott, Dominic J., and Amos Zeichner, "Effects of Hypermasculinity on Physical Aggression Against Women," *Psychology of Men and Masculinity*, Vol. 4, No. 1, January 2003, pp. 70–78.

Paul, Lisa A., and Matt J. Gray, "Sexual Assault Programming on College Campuses: Using Social Psychological Belief and Behavior to Change Principles to Improve Outcomes," *Trauma, Violence, and Abuse*, Vol. 12, No. 2, 2011, pp. 99–109.

Payne, Diana L., Kimberly A. Lonsway, and Louise F. Fitzgerald, "Rape Myth Acceptance: Exploration of Its Structure and Its Measurement Using the Illinois Rape Myth Acceptance Scale," *Journal of Research in Personality*, Vol. 33, No. 1, 1999, pp. 27–68.

Perry, Andrea R., David DiLillo, and James Peugh, "Childhood Psychological Maltreatment and Quality of Marriage: The Mediating Role of Psychological Distress," *Journal of Emotional Abuse*, Vol. 7, No. 2, 2007, pp. 117–142.

Peterson, Zoë D., Emily K. Voller, Melissa A. Polusny, and Maureen Murdoch, "Prevalence and Consequences of Adult Sexual Assault of Men: Review of Empirical Findings and State of the Literature," *Clinical Psychology Review*, Vol. 31, No. 1, 2011, pp. 1–24.

Pino, Nathan W., and Robert F. Meier, "Gender Differences in Rape Reporting," *Sex Roles*, Vol. 40, Nos. 11/12, 1999, pp. 979–990.

Porter, Louise, "Leadership and Role-Taking in Multiple Perpetrator Rape," in Miranda A. H. Horvath and Jessica Woodhams, eds., *Handbook on the Study of Multiple Perpetrator Rape: A Multidisciplinary Response to an International Problem*, New York: Routledge, 2013, pp. 160–181.

Porter, Louise E., and Laurence J. Alison, "A Partially Ordered Scale of Influence in Violent Group Behavior: An Example from Gang Rape," *Small Group Research*, Vol. 32, No. 4, August 2001, pp. 475–497.

———, "Examining Group Rape: A Descriptive Analysis of Offender and Victim Behaviour," *European Journal of Criminology*, Vol. 3, No. 3, 2006, pp. 357–381.

Rand, Michael, and Shannan Catalano, *National Crime Victimization Survey*, Washington, D.C.: Bureau of Justice Statistics, United States Department of Justice, 2006.

Rebocho, Maria Francisca, and Patrícia Silva, "Target Selection in Rapists: The Role of Environmental and Contextual Factors," *Aggression and Violent Behavior*, Vol. 19, 2014, pp. 42–49.

Reidy, Dennis E., Steven D. Shirk, Colleen A. Sloan, and Amos Zeichner, "Men Who Aggress Against Women: Effects of Feminine Gender Role Violation on Physical Aggression in Hypermasculine Men," *Psychology of Men and Masculinity*, Vol. 10, No. 1, 2009, pp. 1–12.

Rice, Marnie E., Terry C. Chaplin, Grant T. Harris, and Joanne Coutts, "Empathy for the Victim and Sexual Arousal Among Rapists and Nonrapists," *Journal of Interpersonal Violence*, Vol. 9, No. 4, 1994, pp. 435–449.

Rock, Lindsay, *2012 Workplace and Gender Relations Survey of Active Duty Members, Survey Note No. 2013–007*, Alexandria, Va.: Human Resources Strategic Assessment Program (HRSAP), Defense Manpower Data Center, March 15, 2013.

Sadler, Anne G., Brenda M. Booth, Brian L. Cook, and Bradley N. Doebbeling, "Factors Associated with Women's Risk of Rape in the Military Environment," *American Journal of Industrial Medicine*, Vol. 43, No. 3, 2003, pp. 262–273.

Senn, Charlene Y., Serge Desmarais, Norine Verberg, and Eileen Wood, "Predicting Coercive Sexual Behavior Across the Lifespan in a Random Sample of Canadian Men," *Journal of Social and Personal Relationships*, Vol. 17, No. 1, 2000, pp. 95–113.

Simbayi, Leickness C., Seth C. Kalichman, Sean Jooste, Vuyisile Mathiti, Demetria Cain, and Charsey Cherry, "HIV/AIDS Risks Among South African Men Who Report Sexually Assaulting Women," *American Journal of Health Behavior*, Vol. 30, No. 2, March/April 2006, pp. 158–166.

Simons, Dominique, Sandy K. Wurtele, and Peggy Heil, "Childhood Victimization and Lack of Empathy as Predictors of Sexual Offending Against Women and Children," *Journal of Interpersonal Violence*, Vol. 17, No. 12, December 2002, pp. 1291–1307.

Smallbone, Stephen W., and Mark R. Dadds, "Attachment and Coercive Sexual Behavior," *Sexual Abuse: A Journal of Research and Treatment*, Vol. 12, No. 1, 2000, pp. 3–15.

Smith, Dave, and Sally Stewart, "Sexual Aggression and Sports Participation," *Journal of Sport Behavior*, Vol. 26, No. 4, 2003, pp. 384–395.

Stander, Valerie A., Lex L. Merrill, Cynthia J. Thomsen, Julie L. Crouch, and Joel S. Milner, "Premilitary Adult Sexual Assault Victimization and Perpetration in a Navy Recruit Sample," *Journal of Interpersonal Violence*, Vol. 23, No. 11, November 2008, pp. 1636–1653.

Stermac, Lana E., Janice A. Du Mont, and Valery Kalemba, "Comparison of Sexual Assaults by Strangers and Known Assailants in an Urban Population of Women," *CMAJ: Canadian Medical Association Journal*, Vol. 153, No. 8, October 1995, pp. 1089–1094.

Stermac, Lana, Peter M. Sheridan, Alison Davidson, and Sheila Dunn, "Sexual Assault of Adult Males," *Journal of Interpersonal Violence*, Vol. 11, No. 1, March 1996, pp. 52–64.

Struckman-Johnson, Cindy, David Struckman-Johnson, and Peter Anderson, "Tactics of Sexual Coercion: When Men and Women Won't Take No for an Answer," *The Journal of Sex Research*, Vol. 40, No. 1, 2003, pp. 76–86.

Suarez, Eliana, and Tahana M. Gadalla, "Stop Blaming the Victim: A Meta-Analysis on Rape Myths," *Journal of Interpersonal Violence*, Vol. 25, No. 11, January 2010, pp. 2010–2035.

Swartout, Kevin M., and Jacquelyn W. White, "The Relationship Between Drug Use and Sexual Aggression in Men Across Time," *Journal of Interpersonal Violence*, Vol. 25, No. 9, January 2010, pp. 1716–1735.

Teicher, Martin, Jacqueline Samson, Ann Polcari, and Cynthia McGreenery, "Sticks, Stones, and Hurtful Words: Relative Effects of Various Forms of Childhood Maltreatment," *American Journal of Psychiatry*, Vol. 163, No. 6, June 2006, pp. 993–1000.

Terry, Karen, *Sexual Offenses and Offenders: Theory, Practice, and Policy*, Boston: Cengage Learning, 2012.

Testa, Maria, and Kurt H. Dermen, "The Differential Correlates of Sexual Coercion and Rape," *Journal of Interpersonal Violence*, Vol. 14, No. 5, May 1999, pp. 548–561.

Tharp, Andra Teten, Sarah DeGue, Linda Anne Valle, Kathryn A. Brookmeyer, Greta M. Massetti, and Jennifer L. Matjasko, "A Systematic Qualitative Review of Risk and Protective Factors for Sexual Violence Perpetration," *Trauma, Violence, and Abuse*, Vol. 14, No. 2, April 2013, pp. 133–167.

Thompson M., M. Koss, J. Kingree, J. Goree, and J. Rice, "A Prospective Mediational Model of Sexual Aggression Among College Men," *Journal of Interpersonal Violence*, Vol. 26, No. 13, September 2011, pp. 2716–2734.

Tjaden, Patricia Godeke, and Nancy Thoennes, *Extent, Nature, and Consequences of Rape Victimization: Findings from the National Violence Against Women Survey*, Washington, D.C.: National Institute of Justice, Office of Justice Programs, U.S. Department of Justice, 2006.

Turchik, Jessica A., and Susan M. Wilson, "Sexual Assault in the U.S. Military: A Review of the Literature and Recommendations for the Future," *Aggression and Violent Behavior*, Vol. 15, 2010, pp. 267–277.

Tyler, Kimberly A., "Social and Emotional Outcomes of Childhood Sexual Abuse: A Review of Recent Research," *Aggression and Violent Behavior*, Vol. 7, No. 6, November/December 2002, pp. 567–589.

Ullman, Sarah E., "A Comparison of Gang and Individual Rape Incidents," *Violence and Victims*, Vol. 14, No. 2, 1999a, pp. 123–133.

———, "Social Support and Recovery from Sexual Assault: A Review," *Aggression and Violent Behavior*, Vol. 4, No. 3, January 1999b, pp. 343–358.

Ullman, Sarah E., and Leanne R. Brecklin, "Alcohol and Adult Sexual Assault in a National Sample of Women," *Journal of Substance Abuse*, Vol. 11, No. 4, 2000, pp. 405–420.

Vandiver, Donna M., "Female Sex Offenders: A Comparison of Solo Offenders and Co-Offenders," *Violence and Victims,* Vol. 21, No. 2, June 2006, pp. 339–354.

Vandiver, Donna M., and Glen Kercher, "Offender and Victim Characteristics of Registered Female Sexual Offenders in Texas: A Proposed Typology of Female Sexual Offenders,"

Sexual Abuse: A Journal of Research and Treatment, Vol. 16, No 2, April 2004, pp. 121–137.

Vega, Vanessa, and Neil M. Malamuth, "Predicting Sexual Aggression: The Role of Pornography in the Context of General and Specific Risk Factors," *Aggressive Behavior*, Vol. 33, No. 2, March/April 2007, pp. 104–117.

Vivolo-Kantor, Alana M., Sarah DeGue, David DiLillo, and Lorraine E. Cuadra, "The Mediating Effect of Hostility Toward Women on the Relationship Between Childhood Emotional Abuse and Sexual Violence Perpetration," *Violence and Victims*, Vol. 28, No. 1, February 2013, pp. 178–191.

Ward, Tony, Stephen M. Hudson, William L. Marshall, and Richard Siegert, "Attachment Style and Intimacy Deficits in Sexual Offenders: A Theoretical Framework," *Sexual Abuse: A Journal of Research and Treatment*, Vol. 7, No. 4, October 1995, pp. 317–335.

Wheeler, Jennifer G., William H. George, and Barbara J. Dahl, "Sexually Aggressive College Males: Empathy as a Moderator in the 'Confluence Model' of Sexual Aggression," *Personality and Individual Differences*, Vol. 33, No. 5, October 2002, pp. 759–775.

White, Jacquelyn W., Darcy McMullin, Kevin Swartout, Stacy Sechrist, and Ashlyn Gollehon, "Violence in Intimate Relationships: A Conceptual and Empirical Examination of Sexual and Physical Aggression," *Children and Youth Services Review*, Vol. 30, No. 3, March 2008, pp. 338–351.

White, Jacquelyn W., and Paige Hall Smith, "Sexual Assault Perpetration and Re-Perpetration from Adolescence to Young Adulthood," *Criminal Justice and Behavior*, Vol. 31, No. 2, 2004, pp. 182–202.

Widom, Cathy Spatz, "Child Abuse and Neglect," in Susan O. White, ed., *Handbook of Youth and Justice*, New York: Kluwer Academic, 2001, pp. 31–47.

Widom, Cathy Spatz, and M. Ashley Ames, "Criminal Consequences of Childhood Sexual Victimization," *Child Abuse and Neglect*, Vol. 18, No. 4, April 1994, pp. 303–318.

Widom, Cathy Spatz, and Robin L. Shepard, "Accuracy of Adult Recollections of Childhood Victimization: Part 1. Childhood Physical Abuse," *Psychological Assessment*, Vol. 8, No. 4, December 1996, pp. 412–421.

Woodhams, Jessica, and Claire Cooke, "Suspect Aggression and Victim Resistance in Multiple Perpetrator Rapes," *Archives of Sexual Behavior*, Vol. 42, No. 8, November 2013, pp. 1509–1516.

Woodhams, Jessica, Claire Cooke, Leigh Harkins, and Teresa da Silva, "Leadership in Multiple Perpetrator Stranger Rape," *Journal of Interpersonal Violence*, Vol. 27, No. 4, March 2012, pp. 728–752.

Woods, Laura, and Louise Porter, "Examining the Relationship Between Sexual Offenders and Their Victims: Interpersonal Differences Between Stranger and Non-Stranger Sexual Offences," *Journal of Sexual Aggression*, Vol. 14, No. 1, March 2008, pp. 61–75.

Yescavage, Karen, "Teaching Women a Lesson: Sexually Aggressive and Sexually Nonaggressive Men's Perceptions of Acquaintance and Date Rape," *Violence Against Women*, Vol. 5, No. 7, July 1999, pp. 796–812.

Zawacki, Tina, Antonia Abbey, Philip O. Buck, Pamela McAuslan, and A. Monique Clinton-Sherrod, "Perpetrators of Alcohol-Involved Sexual Assaults: How Do They Differ from Other Sexual Assault Perpetrators and Nonperpetrators?" *Aggressive Behavior*, Vol. 29, No. 4, August 2003, pp. 366–380.

Zinzow, Heidi M., and Martie Thompson, "A Longitudinal Study of Risk Factors for Repeated Sexual Coercion and Assault in U.S. College Men," *Archives of Sexual Behavior*, Vol. 44, No. 1, 2014, pp. 1–10.